COUPLES IN CRISIS

GW00402183

COUPLES IN CRISIS

Does Your Relationship Have a Future?

CHRIS BELSHAW AND MICHAEL STRUTT

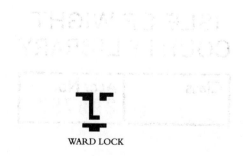

WARD LOCK

A WARD LOCK BOOK

First published in the UK 1984
by Victor Gollancz Ltd
This revised edition published 1996
by Ward Lock
Wellington House, 125 Strand, LONDON WC2R 0BB

A Cassell Imprint

Copyright © Chris Belshaw and Michael Strutt 1984, 1987, 1996

Distributed in the United States
by Sterling Publishing Co., Inc.
387 Park Avenue South, New York, NY 10016–8810

A British Library Cataloguing in Publication Data block for this book may be
obtained from the British Library

ISBN 0 7063 7467 3
Typeset in Linotron Meridien by Business Color Print, Welshpool, Powys
Printed and bound in Great Britain by
Biddles Ltd, Guildford and Kings Lynn

Contents

Acknowledgements

It is only by writing a book that you appreciate all the help that is needed to produce one that is worthwhile. We thank the many people who helped us generously and with whom we were able to explore our ideas. We are particularly grateful to those who were willing to share their personal experiences. Our special thanks go to: Rosemary Russell, who suggested improvements and encouraged us; Renate Olins and Pam Tyler both read the manuscript and offered much helpful advice; Evelyn Hunter, who guided and edited our efforts from the beginning; Maggie Belshaw, who made pertinent contributions and typed some early drafts; Desmond Biddulph read our Dynamics chapter and checked our understanding of psychology; Benedict Birnberg, and Richard Sax of the Solicitors Family Law Association, for checking our legal terms; John Cornwell clarified the work of a divorce solicitor; Leo Abse MP gave us encouragement and explained the background to changing legislation; Caroline and Chris Dorling and Greta Martens for their contributions; Elizabeth Hedgecock, whose patient re-typing of our many drafts was invaluable and who made her own contributions to the book; Pat Blake for providing photocopying facilities when we most needed them.

We are very grateful to the many busy people who generously helped us when we revised the book for this new edition. We particularly want to thank Christopher Vincent, senior marital therapist and clinical lecturer at the Tavistock Marital Studies Institute, London, who suggested valuable research avenues.

For explaining the work of family lawyers we thank: Wendy Beauchamp-Ward, of Tibber Beauchamp-Ward; Sara Robinson, SFLA press officer, and David Hodson (who efficiently checked our legal terms), both of Family Law Consortium, Britain's first law practice

to combine family lawyers. mediators and counsellors. Also staff at
the Council for Family Proceedings, Bristol.

For information and explanations of the mediation process, we are
grateful to: Peter Bailey; Alan Campbell of Perth Family Court
Counselling Service, Western Australia; Linda Fisher of Relationships
Australia, NSW; Thelma Fisher of National Family Mediation; Ruth
Hindley, administrative director, FMA; Jacky Renouf of Relationship
Services New Zealand; Joan Kelly, of Northern California Mediation
Center; Michael J McManus of Marriage Savers' Institute; Susan
Matheson, director, Louise Halliday and staff of Family Mediation
Scotland; Maura Wall Murphy, co-ordinator, Family Mediation
Service, Dublin; Lisa Parkinson, Family Mediators Association (FMA)
founder and trainer; Richard Walker, senior family court welfare
officer, North East London Family Court Welfare Service; Michael
Williams; Paul Young, executive director, Family Mediation Canada.

Emi Karlsson, of Östersund Family Counselling Bureau, Brita
Eketgall of Swedish Church Family Counselling, and staff at the
Swedish Institute gave us information on Sweden's counselling
services. Philip Kirby, counsellor at News International, London,
explained workplace counselling; Bruce Liddington, chairman of
Families Need Fathers; Fiona Price, of Fiona Price and Partners,
London, guided us on independent financial advice. John Quarrell
explained UK pension implications.

For reading parts of our text or proofs we thank Derek Hill, head
of counselling at Relate Marriage Guidance, and Suzy Powling,
communications director; Evelyn Hunter, the Rev. Dick Morris, Iris
Nutting of ICIS, Howard Stacey and Anna Quirke of The Simkins
Partnership. Our thanks also to Emma Baatz, and Ruth Palmer of
Relate, for their encouragement and practical help.

Preface

This book was the result of a chance meeting in the early 1980s. As we talked, we discovered that our separate experiences of marriage breakdown amounted to a body of knowledge we wanted to share with others who could benefit. We decided to combine our resources and *Couples in Crises*, now fully revised and updated, was the result.

It is very much the product of our own experience and that of others who have faced relationship difficulties or worked towards constructive divorce.

Many fascinating changes in attitudes to relationships have taken place in the past decade. Laws have changed too, putting more onus on couples to work out their own solutions. We have included much new material, yet our essential message remains the same.

The book is, foremost, for the ordinary reader. We have widely researched the strategies and techniques used by leading professionals such as counsellors, lawyers and mediators in helping their clients. This has enabled us to include vital information that will aid anyone facing a breakdown in their relationship.

For professionals, the book offers a reference source and a view of best practice their clients will meet in other disciplines.

The law varies from country to country; where we discuss it in detail, we refer to England and Wales. Legal terms are explained in everyday language in a separate list.

The reader is urged to seek information and professional advice where necessary.

Introduction

No one needs to be told how painful the breakdown of a marriage or longstanding relationship can be for all but a fortunate few. Often we wish afterwards that things could have worked out differently. It can be a very long time before we are able to regain our usual spirits, or be convinced that life can return to some sort of normality.

The message of this book is that in many relationships – and we hope in yours – there is much you can do to help yourself. We are sure that a book can help in these sensitive circumstances. A stressful relationship need *not* slide out of control. If you are in the traumatic stage that so often precedes a break-up, there is much you can do to prevent misunderstandings from getting out of hand and to express your own upset constructively. At the same time it is possible, if you divorce, to create a very positive basis for staying on reasonable terms with your partner and this is particularly important where there are children. If you have split up or divorced, there are still ways of handling the situation which can bring increased peace of mind in the long run, even if your partner will not co-operate.

What we advocate is an approach to these difficulties which can make it easier for you to cope with the practical and emotional problems. At the same time, it can transform the relationship with your partner into a positive one for as long as you remain in touch. It involves a willingness to be patient, understanding and collected about what either of you wants; to solve problems that arise in a way which will preserve, and even build up, self-respect and care and respect for each other. You may not feel like this but couples who have made the effort – often reluctantly at first – have found that it makes life easier eventually. We give information to help resolve conflict and improve understanding. We don't offer a complete answer or 'method' for dealing with breakdown but suggest ways of working with the situation to find your own solutions. This will enable you to consider other points of view and anticipate some problems before they arise.

Lacking the experience and practice that makes us skilful in other areas of life, we find it hard to handle the issues and upsets when a marriage or live-in relationship goes wrong. And because it is so often traumatic, very many people can do no more than flounder through an extended period of months, even years, in which many emotions are aroused and their whole life is turned upside down. But there are skills involved which can be learned and ways of applying them which bring results beneficial to both adults and children. The approach that we describe in the following chapters can help you deal with anger, guilt, bitterness and a sense of loss. It may also keep you sane, and even cheerful, at times when things are black. It could save you time and money, too.

But beware. Because your pride, your self-esteem, your insecurities and your ability to see life from other points of view will all be tested, it is likely to prove anything but easy to put what we have to say into practice at first. To face a breakdown positively, as we suggest, may demand of you more patience, tact, forgiveness and forbearance than you thought you had. You may exasperate relatives, puzzle your friends and anger your partner. You may find yourself examining your motives and your relationships with others in a way you never have before. It may force even more heart-searching about what you and your partner have wanted from each other and what you want in life for yourself. And you may wonder at times – perhaps when your attempts to communicate are met by abuse or indifference – whether it is all worth the bother. If you find yourself in similar difficulties in another relationship or a second marriage, it is likely to be no less painful.

Even with today's high rates of divorce, marriage remains very popular. In the UK, the divorce rate for England and Wales is still among the highest in Europe at about one in three, involving about 160,000 couples a year, while that in the United States is even higher: about 50 per cent of American marriages end in the divorce court. People who live together without marriage face similar insecurity even when they have children.

The high proportion of couples cohabiting in many countries (though they may marry at a later stage) is something statistics can take little real account of, leaving a great deal of guesswork about this trend. In Sweden, 50 per cent of children are born outside marriage, with about a quarter to one-third in the UK, France and Austria. 'Cohabiting unions tend to be short-term and child-free. They last about two years on average, and either convert into marriage or break up,' according to the sociologist Ceridwen Roberts (1995).

Why these trends should affect so many societies no one is sure, but a number of reasons have been put forward. We would point to the progressive emancipation of women since the mid-nineteenth century which led to the divorce peak after the Second World War – a period when greater equality was made necessary by the war effort. Also, war experiences changed people's perceptions of themselves.

It is no easier in a second, or third, marriage. This was recognised in the early 1980s when Gwynn Davis, a social scientist, speaking of the English legal system, said:

> The whole tenor of matrimonial proceedings is to a large extent determined by solicitors and they are responsible for translating their clients' problems into legal terms and also advising them to the limits within which they can operate in this framework. Since the client has no point of comparison, it is difficult for him to question the way in which his situation is interpreted. The solicitor therefore has considerable control over the route that is pursued
>
> (Davis, 1982)

He continued:

> There has been little attempt to explore the element of common ground between husband and wife, or to mobilise the couple's sense of fairness which need not cease when the marriage breaks down. Much of the blame for this imbalance has been attached to aggressive solicitors who, it is said, inflame the conflict. But solicitors are bound by the system within which they operate. The procedure is not designed to cater for the interests of the family as a whole.

His comments reflected a common experience in many Western countries at the time.

Some American research on the subject seems to point to a close correlation between the rise in jobs for women and the increase in the divorce rate. This may be only a partial explanation, however. It can be argued that because married women are at work in greater numbers than ever before, they now have the same chance that men have always had to compare their lives with others. And it is no longer socially unacceptable to have sex without marriage.

The women's movement has been a powerful factor in enabling women to become more independent, and it has given confidence to many who want to have careers as well as, or instead of, bringing up a family. Accordingly, women are in a much stronger position than they have ever been to judge when a relationship is empty and so more willing and better equipped to establish a life that has more meaning for them. Indeed, many seem to be doing just that. Figures in the UK and America show that up to two-thirds of divorces are initiated by women.

The fear for people who split up or divorce is the feeling that events are outside their control, perhaps for the first time in their life. And this can be brought home when they enter the legal process and encounter the machinery which governs the legal side of ending a marriage. People feel vulnerable and unprepared in a situation in which they may already be upset, angry or very worried.

Fortunately much has changed in recent years. A revised legal framework in countries around the world has created a climate in which lawyers are encouraged not to act adversarially. The new systems aim to reduce conflict and the court's role in imposing solutions. In addition, an increasing number of lawyers are training to join the mediation services. We look at the value of mediation in this book.

Breaking up, especially where children are involved, is a complex experience which has no sense or meaning if it provides freedom only at the expense of much upset and disillusion. What it does represent is change at a personal level. Whatever else can be said about it, nearly everyone will agree that if there is a break-up, this represents a dramatic alteration in a person's life. Such change is often regarded as disastrous but we need not take a negative view – change can be positive and we emphasise this throughout the book.

The idea of change being a process is one you will meet again and again in the chapters that follow. And, because you are involved in the process of change, you may have to make some tough decisions.

At a turning point, it takes courage of a particular kind to get to the heart of difficult issues in a relationship and rebuild it for the future. It takes courage of another kind to act on the realisation that a relationship which has no future must be given up. Decisions like these are hard but they may be demanded of us if we are to learn and develop in life.

The circumstances surrounding breakdown and divorce always contain a message, a commentary on our ability to relate closely to another person. If we allow, it provides insights into ourselves – and usually tells us something we need to know. The breakdown of a marriage is often talked about by marriage 'experts' as if it were some kind of illness, and in a way it is. It is a period when the powerful emotional and irrational side of human nature takes over and colours everything we feel and do. It is hard to explain much of what is done and said in any other terms.

More accurately, it is a journey of transformation at an inner level which a person can either co-operate with or ignore. One which can equip you to meet life with greater maturity and in better shape than before. Set aside any assumptions you may have: there are many views and myths about breakdown and divorce and you will experience it in your own way.

CHAPTER ONE

Dynamics of Relationships

How we choose our partners

'I'm very glad she's marrying so promptly,' said Mrs Cocks. 'I do believe in girls marrying young. Of course, she's very young; only just eighteen. But it's so much easier and wiser for them to marry before they form their tastes too much, don't you think?'

Margaret Kennedy – The Ladies of Lydon

We choose our partners for many and varied reasons. Some are obvious. We may be attracted to someone who has similar interests or who has an attractive manner. They may dress in an interesting way, share a sense of humour which makes them fun to be with, or have a similar family background so that we feel particularly comfortable with them. Or, conversely, they may be totally different to anyone else we have ever met and this is the attraction. We might be bowled over by a person's intelligence or their talents, or there may be a closely matched religious background. Behind our choice is often self-interest in the form of security, money, position or safety. We may even choose out of pity. And, not least, sexual attraction may cut across all the differences so that nothing else seems to matter.

The reasons that make us want to be with a particular person – whether to marry or live with them – vary infinitely from one individual to another but somehow we mostly make a choice we feel will suit us. Of course the way we make that choice varies too, so that sometimes it seems less of a choice than we realise. We may even feel that we don't choose at all, that circumstances made us fall in love with a person to whom our destiny is linked. Or, in retrospect, we may acknowledge that family pressure to marry someone because they would be a good match, and good relations with the family depend on it, persuaded us to go along with the idea, a choice we might otherwise not have made.

Choice comes in another guise in arranged Asian marriages, where the partners are selected by the two families, and the prospective couple, who may never have met, are expected to go along with that decision. It is revealing that the reactions of the two people involved can vary from warm agreement to outright refusal, by one or both. The Asian idea that the family is in a better position to choose a partner for a son or daughter because it has more experience to judge whether it would be a good match emotionally and economically has something to be said for it. By comparison, the Western premise is that a person chooses a partner for him or herself because that is exercising individual freedom, but then they may choose badly and have to divorce. So if a Western person goes along with a family's wishes and stays married for many years, while an Asian refuses to marry his family's choice, as happens among young Asians living in Europe, then conformity or otherwise goes beyond cultural patterns.

Thus it is worth commenting here that if two people whose marriage has been arranged by Asian families can stay happily married for many years, as is often the case, then free choice – the Western criterion – is far from being necessarily as desirable as it appears.

What makes us create partnerships above and beyond culture are needs we all recognize: the need for a home, for love and affection, sexual fulfilment, and for most of us the urge to bear children. We also need emotional security and appreciation of our worth.

What has all this to do with love, which in the West is regarded as the basis of marriage? Erich Fromm (1975) says this: 'To love somebody is not just a strong feeling – it is a decision, it is a judgement, it is a promise.'

It is from this starting point that we want to go on to show the drives in all of us which we believe are fundamentally responsible for the choices we make in our partners, and why our feelings and judgements change. And it is from here that we will reach our main theme.

People as they really are

Most of us present a face to the world, even to those who know us intimately, which may be only a part of ourselves. We are taught to believe this is how we are: that Mary is cheerful, friendly, self-reliant; that John is moody, taciturn and stubborn; and that Uncle George is always in a dream but fun really when you get to know him. It is true that we will often go further than this and say, for example, that Mary is occasionally impatient with people and sometimes gets depressed and that John can be very forthcoming and perceptive if he is in the right mood; and that Uncle George has a way with animals that you wouldn't believe.

But somehow we still do not know the real person. How is it that Mary suddenly ran off to live with a layabout who seems to care nothing for her? What is it in John that attracts so many oddball friends when he surely isn't like that; and why did Uncle George stay forty years in his job at the Gas Board when he has so many talents?

Appearances are deceptive and we are limited by our perceptions. Why, even the people we live with and may have married thirty years ago are baffling at times.

Psychologists and psychiatrists are still arguing about the underlying complexities and contradictions in human nature and, in the meantime, the rest of us have to do the best we can with the knowledge we have. Some people are aware, for example, of having more than one personality. The singer Eartha Kitt once said her powerful stage persona was totally different to her off-stage manner and that she thoroughly enjoyed being the different person she was while performing. In other people these 'sub-personalities' come to light fleetingly, as when someone who is normally quiet changes and becomes the life and soul of a party; or during exercises in personal development groups. Ike Turner, the American musician, is said to have expressed this kind of reality too.

> 'Ike', one of his close friends said, 'once told me that there are two people in his head. There is Ike Turner, and another guy he calls Willy. Willy is the decent, sensitive person who can be very easily hurt. And when Willy is in danger of being hurt, that's when Ike comes out, to take care of business.'

(Independent Magazine, *October 1995*)

As individuals we vary enormously in our maturity, judgement, skills, aspirations and capacity to love; this is what makes the world such a diverse and fascinating place. We relate to others with whom we work, live or play in many different ways, conditioned to a great degree by our childhood experiences. A child from a loving family which cherishes affection, and fosters confidence and a sense of humour, is much more likely, when grown up, to seek a mate with similar qualities no matter how their personalities may differ, and make a relationship which will bring out the best in both. Between them, they will have a lot in reserve to deal with any difficulties. In contrast, a child who is constantly abused and put down and whose talents are denied will probably grow up suspicious and fearful. He will have little chance of making mature relationships unless he changes considerably.

Most of us are born into families which fall between these two extremes, but that doesn't make it any easier. We may have come from a home where there was both love and hatred in the air simultaneously; where one parent loved the children and the other was cold or absent. There may have been a home atmosphere where problems were shared and openly discussed, or one where everything was kept behind closed doors. Our parents may have been outgoing and taught us a healthy curiosity or they may have had little to teach that would enable us to get on in the world. Somehow, we have had to learn what we could during our childhood and make the best of it when we grow up and are put to the tests of adulthood.

To some extent this makes us victims or beneficiaries of the luck of the draw but how does this help us if we have pulled a shorter straw than others? We have within us drives and talents which are unique to each of us and these can be distorted or reinforced according to our experiences as we grow up. Most of the time we are content to let these problems lie – or at least the manifestations of them. So it is that we accept that I have a bad temper, that you are never on time, that Joe cannot hold down a job. Yet these are symptoms of the distortion we have been talking about. If Jim hasn't got a bad temper but loses it only when there is good justification, what has he got that I cannot learn? If Lucy is usually on time except when the traffic is bad, whan can you learn from her? And what is it that makes Joe leave one job after another?

People are as they are. Or are they? To become an adult in the true sense is not to be faultless but to function effectively and use our talents as far as we are able. And those talents include being able to relate as successfully as we can to those near to us and those we work with.

Opportunities for change

Far from standing still emotionally and psychologically as adults, we are sent new challenges to add to those of childhood and adolescence. This is widely recognised by many psychologists, teachers and clergy, doctors and others, but until recently was almost ignored by people in general. We prefer to feel comfortable with the idea that by the age of twenty-five or so, we have reached maturity and events in adult life such as bereavement, problems at work, problems with children, and divorce, are mostly bad luck or difficulties to be shrugged off as getting in the way of normality.

Instead, the truth is that we are being challenged to learn and develop still further as adults, often more than in the emotionally turbulent teenage years.

The final test, of course, is old age and death, for which, some think, our lives can be seen as a preparation.

There are many examples of people's lives being changed by difficult experiences as well as pleasant ones, and our mistakes, trials and even our illnesses all offer a way to learn and develop. To suffer without learning from the experience is to waste the experience. What is more, it can invite its recurrence and this can be seen to hold true in relationships where, for example, a woman marries or lives with two or even three men in succession, each of whom turns out to be alcoholic, or beats her up. At a subconscious level she is repeatedly making the same choice.

> Janet married young, at twenty-one, and had a very argumentative and sometimes violent relationship with John. They divorced ten years later and Janet is now seeing Richard. They have talked of living together but Janet, understandably perhaps, wishes to stay free for the time being, and be able to see other men. Richard resents this and has also begun turning up at her home just when he feels like it. They have had some

bitter arguments about this, with Richard getting very heated about the subject of other men. Now Janet is having doubts about continuing the relationship but hopes that somehow things will resolve themselves.

At the back of her mind Janet has the feeling that Richard may well be impossible to live with even if she were faithful. This situation clearly has some of the ingredients of her marriage and the test, which may be a hard one, is either to solve the problem with Richard or accept that the relationship with him cannot work and has to be given up. If she takes neither course she may well find herself in another very argumentative partnership.

To split up from someone we have lived with for a long time may be necessary and painful, but pain itself, unwelcome though it is, is a part of life we all have to confront at one time or another. The Jesuit writer, John Powell, puts it this way:

> *Pain itself is not evil, to be avoided at all costs. Pain is rather a teacher from whom we can learn much. Pain is instructing us, telling us to change, to stop doing one thing or to begin doing another, to stop thinking one way and begin thinking differently. When we refuse to listen to pain and its lessons . . . in effect we have said: 'I will not listen. I will not learn. I will not change.'*
>
> *(Powell, 1974).*

The events which bring change, whether painful or not, do not happen randomly. They occur, modern psychologists say, at points in our lives when change needs to occur. Therapists almost invariably find that people come to them for help at some point of crisis. A relationship may have broken up or is about to, powerful dreams may have disturbed them, or a business or career collapsed. The therapist will immediately see these events as signs of change or a need for change, signalled from the person's unconscious, and help to make him or her aware of it.

Such change is part of the process of maturing; at whatever age it occurs, it is better that the person be aware of it and able to co-operate with it.

Humanistic psychologists such as C.G. Jung and Roberto Assagioli suggest that events in the everyday world which affect us are outward manifestations of a process going on in the psyche. So that, for example, when we become seriously ill and are forced to stay in bed for a while, it may be that we are subconsciously giving ourselves the time to take stock of ourselves or some situation which normally we stay too busy to consider.

The change in our lives required could be a practical one, perhaps compelling the hard businessman, if he will listen, to slow down and find a vocation which will bring out his artistic qualities. Or the thoughtless person may subconsciously attract some sharp raps on the knuckles which, if he listens, will suggest that he become more sensitive to others' needs. This may seem too subtle but we readily accept the principle when it is demonstrated in a way as obvious as this: a salesman who drove everywhere recklessly in his high-powered car quite clearly was heading for an awful crash, particularly when two minor collisions and a near miss made no difference to his driving style. When it came, the salesman collided head-on with another car and killed the two people in it as well as himself.

The important point we want to emphasise in this section is that we are much more complex beings than we are taught to believe and we often have less real control over our lives than we like to imagine. One reason for this is that our upbringing and education tend to train people into roles rather than help them express their true individuality, right down to the level – as the feminists have shown – that sexual stereotyping has poisoned the natural and healthy relationship between men and women. While the most extreme feminists almost seem to want the present bias replaced by a reverse tyranny, in which men would be in some way subservient to women, the principal point that there is an imbalance indoctrinated into most men holds true.

It can be very difficult to disentangle roles and attitudes from what our true values and feelings might be if we were not subject to such conditioning. But being aware of it is a start.

A second reason, as C.G. Jung showed, is that we all grow up with biases in our psychological makeup which leave us incomplete, so that throughout our lives we learn to express those parts of ourselves through others. And to return to the theme of this book, this applies most particularly to the partners with whom we choose to live.

In a marriage which works well each partner can help the other express some, and perhaps many, of these qualities which our role-

21

playing does not allow us to bring forward, because close relationships must go beyond roles to work at more than a surface, social level. A couple that is complementary in this way, with both parties willing to cast roles aside and learn from each other, can help to bring out such latent qualities. It is a joy to watch a couple who relate well act in a truly complementary way, listening to each other, helping each other along.

However, sometimes couples get together who are not complementary but are polarised. That is, each one has an overabundance of some quality that in the other may be lying totally undeveloped.

> David and Joan married in their twenties but argued constantly almost from the moment they met. Though they were strongly attracted to each other physically, there seemed to be nothing that they did together which could not trigger an argument. Eventually they divorced. What they discovered in the process of marriage guidance counselling was that David, primarily a thinker, functioned almost entirely through his mind and was unable to respond to Joan's feelings. And Joan, who had missed out on her education but had very strong and often un-controlled feelings, could not relate at all to David's verbal approach to everything. Each has since had to work on their hidden, unreached function which will give them a better chance in other relationships.

This brings us to an important point we want to make in this chapter: that we are not simply mind, or feelings, or bodies. All are equally necessary vehicles for self-expression and communication. We may each have a bias towards one or another and there is nothing wrong in this but if we over-use one at the expense of the other two, we are in trouble. In John Powell's words:

> *Man is not simple. He is composed of body, mind and spirit and he has needs on all three levels of his existence. He has needs and appetites that are physical, psychological and spiritual. Frustration at any one of these levels can produce agony in the whole organism*
>
> *(Powell, 1974).*

A diagram may help to show these three areas, all of which must function so that we can operate successfully in the everyday world and also enjoy good health.

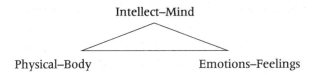

Intellect–Mind

Physical–Body   Emotions–Feelings

These three sides of our nature are within all of us. By using our bodies we explore the world and become close to others; our emotions and feelings enable us to savour experience, to empathise and communicate non-verbally, and our minds can put our experience into a context and help guide us. Together the three create meaning.

What's going on in the psyche

Any relationship between two people will involve the interaction of the two halves of each other's psyche – the conscious and the unconscious – so that in effect four people, not two, are relating to each other. The discovery of the unconscious, the submerged part of our nature over which we have no control, was made by Sigmund Freud at the turn of the century and it is among the most important discoveries of modern times.

Freud established depth psychology as a field worthy of study and his pioneering work was quickly taken up by others, including the Swiss psychiatrist C.G. Jung, who collaborated with him. However, Jung split with Freud in 1911–12 over the theory, fundamental to Freud, that sexuality, and in particular fantasies of incest, are man's dominating instinct. Jung believed there were other crucial factors and, throughout the years until his death in 1961, he carried out an enormous amount of research in many fields to back his view.

The split between Jung and Freud resulted in a rift which even now divides the whole psycho-therapeutic movement, with implications in many areas of life and particularly mental health. We mention this for two reasons. The first is that the Freudian view of human nature is still a predominating one, so that, with its limitations, it is at the basis of the popular view of what is inside our minds. The second is that Jung, in a lifetime of psycho-therapeutic work and diverse scholarship in which he studied ancient texts and religions, primitive peoples and the use of dreams and symbols in many different cultures, went far beyond Freud to produce an astonishingly wide-ranging view of humanity.

Jung's ideas form the basis of this section and, indeed, underlie much of what we have to say throughout this book. The nature of the psyche, which is the totality in which the mind operates, is a huge subject but what we will do here is summarise and simplify *some* of its aspects which are relevant to our theme. Jung's ideas are complex and subtle but we hope, in this highly selective way, to provide insights into how individuals and the relationships they make function in the way they do.

Jung's view was that modern man had become separated from the primitive instinctual side of his nature and that this split was the cause of many problems at both personal and group level, extending even to mass 'illness' such as the rise of Hitler's Reich.

Jung's investigation of these separate functions led him to describe distinct ways in which individual people behave. He also showed that where we do not try consciously to integrate them, our unconscious may act for us instead. It was Jung who coined the terms 'introvert' and 'extrovert' which have become common usage. However, they are not generally used in the way that he meant. The popular view is that an extrovert is someone who is outgoing, plain-speaking and probably easy to get on with, while an introvert keeps to himself, is difficult to make conversation with, and thinks too much. This may be true of some people but it is a crude over-simplification of what Jung had in mind since he was really talking about the way a person experiences life. From this standpoint an extrovert is someone who is completely involved in the world about him, who tries to accept it exactly as it is even if he finds it perplexing at times. He distrusts the idea of having any profound thoughts about himself and accepts the majority view. In contrast the introvert evaluates his experience of the world and ponders on what he finds. To him the world is what he makes of it and not what at first sight it appears to be. His own thoughts are important to him and he is likely to trust them more than he trusts accepted views.

A person tends to be predominantly introvert or predominantly extrovert but normally will combine something of the two, or he may alternate between one or the other depending on what he is doing. For example, someone who tends to be quiet and thoughtful may suddenly become the life and soul of the party after he has had a few drinks and his extrovert side takes over.

Jung also identified and classified a system of character typing which had been in use for centuries and which he called the four functions. There are four distinct ways by which we handle and judge things in everyday life. They are qualities of temperament formed in part by our experiences and in each of us one of them is likely to be more strongly developed than the others. The four functions are Thinking, Feeling, Sensation and Intuition.

The person with Thinking as his main function tends to deal with everything at a logical level. Anything for which there is no logical answer worries him and so he can be completely at sea where his feelings are concerned. The Feeling type is completely at home with his emotions and is able to tune into other people's feelings and attitudes. He dislikes logical responses to everything, being aware that life is not so cut and dried. The Sensation type has a practical, everyday awareness of all that is around him and likes routine. He also likes life to be exactly as it appears to be without questioning or debating what he knows. The person in whom Intuition is dominant operates by hunch for much of the time and seems to pluck ideas from nowhere. He can have the useful knack of spotting the essence of what needs to be done in a situation but, because he does not like routine, he tends to initiate but not follow through where a lot of work is needed.

Jung showed that the four functions work as pairs of opposites, so that Thinking and Feeling, and Sensation and Intuition, are linked. One of the functions in a pair will tend to be predominant at the expense of the other which, therefore, remains unconscious and so inaccessible until we make efforts to balance them. For example, a person who is dominated by his Thinking function may find it hard to cope in a situation where feelings are important, such as a love relationship. And a person who is Sensation dominated may be too concerned with the immediate pleasures of life at the expense of having any regard for the future.

A function which predominates can come in very useful where we use it as a special talent. For instance, the Feeling person may have considerable aptitude for working with other people, or for acting, both of which demand the ability to build up a strong rapport with others. But the less dominant function would still need to be integrated.

The importance of the concept of the four functions is that it provides in part a yardstick with which a particular person can be understood and it also helps us to understand the ways in which we may be different from them.

Jung found, through working with many patients, that another concept about ourselves which had been long known was also valid. This is the idea that each person has a masculine and feminine side to his nature. In a man the masculine instincts are usually the stronger ones and those he is most in touch with. These include the qualities of drive, aggression, rational thinking and a need for goals. In a woman the feminine instincts are usually the ones she identifies with and these include the urge to nurture, receptivity to others, adaptability and thought processes which are intuitive rather than rational, though just as valid.

In a man the masculine drives are part of his conscious self while the feminine side, which Jung called the *anima*, is generally unconscious and needs to be integrated. The feminine in a man relates to values of gentleness, caring and feeling which have to be developed if he is to become a whole person. Similarly, the feminine values are those with which women are consciously in touch as a rule, so that it is the unconscious masculine side, which Jung called the *animus*, which a woman needs to develop if she is to be whole.

Jung showed that the extent to which we are in touch with this unconscious side of ourselves can make a great deal of difference in terms of the personalities of the sexual partners we are attracted to.

The continuing struggle over the roles of men and women in Western society is the result of a clash between increasing awareness and the stereotyped ways in which we are still expected to conform to social norms which do not acknowledge that we have both the masculine and feminine within us. This clash is played out directly in the dissatisfaction people feel in their relationships. We all know the classic situation in childhood when a boy falls down and cuts his knee and then is told by his parents to be grown up and stop crying, while a girl to whom the same thing happens is more often picked up, comforted and allowed to cry. What both need essentially is the parent's acceptance of their pain and some comforting, thus acknowledging the child's feelings.

We tend to divide male and female roles into stereotyped sets of actions and only the most noisy protests of the women's movement have forced the issue into the open – incidentally using women's masculine energies to do it. Although a younger generation has benefited from changing attitudes, such as more equal opportunities at work, the continuing number of sex discrimination cases reaching the courts reveal that old attitudes remain. Very much more progress has to be made if masculine and feminine energies are to be fully expressed and gender stereotyping banished.

Most of us continue to make our relationships on these shaky foundations, full of expectations of what male and female are and are supposed to do while being unaware of the sexual polarity within each of us. But while on a superficial level this crude division seemed to work in Victorian times, with the emancipation of today feelings of anger, resentment and jealousy which build up cannot be dismissed.

How we experience life individually will depend on the combination of all these elements within us, but an important factor is the way we interrelate with others, particularly in close relationships. It is here that a very important psychological mechanism, called *projection*, comes into play. This is an unconscious trick of the mind by which we tend to see in others aspects of our character which we do not want to admit about ourselves. The person who is always accusing others of being difficult and argumentative is often observed to be like this himself. A graphic example is the claim by Hitler in the 1930s that Churchill was a warmonger, rampaging about Europe looking for excuses to start a conflict.

Projection is something we do quite without knowing it and usually it impairs our judgement only in areas where we are vulnerable, such as particular sensitivities or things we feel very strongly about for some reason. Strong emotions are the hallmarks of projection. The best example is that of falling in love. When we fall in love we project on to the other person qualities which are ideals we hold in ourselves, perhaps that of the perfect woman or perfect man. It is when we gradually see the person as they really are, with ordinary human virtues and failings, that we withdraw the projection and have to relate to them as a real person. Sometimes this is very hard, or even impossible, to do because the real person may be very different from what we thought. When two people get down to seeing each other in this way the realisation can be so disillusioning that it may be impossible to continue the relationship.

Projection also reveals itself in other ways. Our unconscious wishes and fears can lead us into circumstances, or to people in our lives, that we least expect. Here are two examples:

> Peter went to a therapist to try to find out why his second marriage was in trouble. His second wife, exactly like the first, had run off to an exciting new man in another country. The therapy brought to light that a hidden and unexpected part of Peter's nature was that of a free-loving adventurer. Being unaware of this he had acted in ways which influenced his wife and she had then acted out what was part of his own nature.

> Martin spent years looking for a gentle, artistic woman with whom he could have a perfect relationship. Instead he constantly found himself with women who appeared charming but turned out to be stubborn and tyrannical. It turned out that his long-forgotten childhood experiences of women had led him always to expect the worst in them, so that at a deep subconscious level he was allowing himself to be attracted to difficult partners instead.

Very often we notice unattractive qualities in other people which in fact are aspects of our own personality which we cannot acknowledge at a conscious level because they do not fit in with our image of ourselves. Projection is equally a factor in qualities we admire in someone else – they are often unexpressed qualities we have ourselves.

Another important idea used in psychology is that of *repression*. Something which is repressed is held in the unconscious so that we are not aware of it at a conscious level. It could be an event or events in childhood or adolescence which have been conveniently 'forgotten' because they were very upsetting. Sometimes, because of the way a person has been brought up, he may repress certain feelings such as affection, tenderness and spontaneity. Most people as they grow up leave some unfortunate memories behind and it is as well that we do, but where our natural behaviour patterns are seriously modified by difficult experiences, this can have its repercussions in adult relationships.

> Mary and Eric married in their early twenties, but it was not successful. Among other problems Mary found Eric unsatisfactory in a way that was a constant undercurrent during their life together, but which Eric only came to understand some time after they separated, when he was persuaded to join a yoga class which included exercises involving the pupils in holding eye contact and touching each other. He realised very quickly that compared with the other people in the class he was extremely inhibited about touching other people and, much later, realised that this inhibition had been at least partly responsible for Mary's attitude towards him. It was a year or two later that he was able to cast his mind back to his childhood and recall, for the first time, that he was constantly being punished for misdemeanors and told to 'shut up'. He noticed too that it was a family pattern that people rarely touched each other, or cuddled, and this was something he felt he had missed.

A variety of experiences can make us repress our normal human responses, making an indelible mark on us. War is one of them as the following example shows. In 1981 four veterans of the Vietnam war became the first Americans to go back to the country since the pull-out by the United States in 1975. A journalist who went with them wrote:

> *On the fifth day we flew south to Saigon, now Ho Chi Minh City, passing over the wasted jungles and fields of dead earth and bomb craters. As we looked down over the newly erected villages and re-cultivated rice paddies I said to Michael Harbert: 'Another veteran once said to me, "I never thought of Vietnam as a country before. It was just a war." Did you feel like that?' Harbert, who knew Vietnam only from the air, had fought a war of almost clinical detachment. 'It wasn't even that for me,' he said. 'It was just a set of co-ordinates.'*

(Observer Magazine, 19 April 1982)

This is an example of how a normally sensitive man can be trained to become the calculating fighting machine that war requires.

Associated with repression is another phenomenon, called *rationalisation*. Rationalisation is where we can find spurious reasons why we do or believe something but will not face the real reason. It allows us to take a course of action or cling to a particular idea or ideas so that we do not have to change, or accept something we do not want. Because it happens unconsciously we genuinely see something in a certain way while everyone we know may be able to see clearly that this is not so. A simple example is the person who stays in the same job long after the time they recognised they should make a move. They ignore these feelings by saying to themselves that the job is stable and secure and it would now be a 'risk' to change.

Another example is the girl who wants to marry a man whom her relatives and friends are certain is not good for her. Some may even point this out but she is in love with him and cannot accept that he has any serious faults. Yes, she does know that he likes to go out drinking several nights a week and he has got into debt. And, yes, she felt terrible after he came home drunk a couple of times and got rough with her. But 'he is a good guy at heart and will settle down when we are married'. That is rationalisation. If they marry and the relationship gets much worse, so that her family have to intervene for her safety, she may then say: 'I should have known what would happen.' Of course, no one could have said for certain that the girl's judgement was wrong, but she wanted things her way while they could see before the marriage that the odds were stacked against her.

Finally, the idea of the 'shadow' side of the personality was introduced by Jung. The *shadow* is the repressed part of our nature, the unpleasant aspects of ourselves which other people can often see but we may be entirely unaware of. It is, therefore, the area where we are most sensitive to other people's criticisms and also where we are emotionally the most vulnerable. Our most sensitive areas are nearly always exposed in close relationships so that when someone steps on our shadow we tend to react strongly – but we could, instead, try to see if they have a point. We become aware of our partner's shadow when we get to know them more deeply after having fallen in love. Once we begin to see that person as they really are, with their share of the failings that all people have, we have to find a way of accepting their faults. Couples who argue a lot are usually experts at treading on each other's shadows as they catalogue each other's failings – they are untidy, they always come in late, they are lazy and so on. But used only as ammunition in a slanging match, this cannot solve anything.

Left unchecked, rationalisation and difficulties in dealing with the shadow can create serious communication problems. Two people who have fixed opinions and ideas about themselves may very often be unable to admit that they are wrong. Instead, they will find all the more reasons why they are right and so, instead of sharing their thoughts and differences honestly, barriers are built up between them. Many stalemate marriages are sustained by this foundation and it may take the rude shock of divorce and new relationships to force change.

However, new-found knowledge that we have of ourselves can be put to work. Once we become aware of where our responses originate, there is an opportunity to change those aspects of ourselves which are not productive. In time, unhelpful habits and attitudes can be discarded, leaving room for more useful ones to take their place.

Patterns of relationship

One of the strongest feelings we have when we fall in love is that being with the other person makes us complete. It is this which gives us the feeling that we 'need' them. Our need for another person can be a very powerful one, but it says as much about our own qualities as those we admire in the person we love. It also reflects what we have experienced or failed to experience in our youth.

As we grow up we learn from our relationships with our parents, friends and relations and this enables us to develop into mature adults. But those aspects of our personality which, as a child, we have not developed – independence, self-reliance and so on – will continue to function on an immature level. Later, when we make relationships as adults, we may be attracted unconsciously to people from whom we can learn about these undeveloped areas of ourselves.

> Harry was twenty-five and Kate twenty when they married. He was happy to take the traditional husband's role as the provider and leader and she was the dutiful wife, making meals and looking after the house. This worked for several years. Kate had little experience of life at large and was happy to get the attention and care of a 'parent' from the willing and helpful Harry. Harry in turn felt that by building his life round doing things for Kate he was doing what a husband is supposed to do.

However, he really wanted to try new interests, travel and lead a lively social life and he felt that Kate blocked many of his ideas like a stubborn child, always complaining how bored she was. They survived an affair by Harry, when he came to the conclusion that a mutual exchange of ideas together with a sharing of sexual expression was missing from the marriage. However, he doggedly did not act on this conviction but continued to try to be the 'good husband and father' since they now also had a child. Kate gradually realised too that this was not the relationship she wanted and embarked on an affair herself. Now she was asserting some of the independence she previously had lacked and Harry's continuing efforts to please her only resulted in his being pushed further and further away. When, after Kate's affair had lasted for three years it became clear to Harry that things were not going to change, they agreed to divorce.

The real person is often behind the person you fall in love with – the one we cannot see when we are in love – and it may take a relationship as close and committed as marriage to bring out the real person in both partners. It is a process which could take two years or twenty depending on their level of maturity to start with and what lies dormant within them. Again, it will also depend on their circumstances and the nature of their relationship if and when this is triggered. Sometimes it never happens.

Two people in a close relationship can influence each other in subtle and positive ways, so that each can learn from the other and develop those aspects which still need to mature. This is one of the hallmarks of a successful relationship whether it lasts a lifetime or not. Through living together the partners can each learn behaviour patterns that are outside their own experience and so become a more complete person – complete in the sense that Jung meant when he talked about wholeness. Dr Paul Tournier, another Swiss psychiatrist, put it another way when he said: 'No one can develop freely in this world and find a full life without feeling understood by one person' (Powell, 1975).

We search for this completeness throughout relationships but there are limits. Where two people come together who are reasonably evenly developed they are likely to have a complementary relationship with the give and take this involves. It can be successful for a long time. But if, instead, they are polarised psychologically, then they may be too different from each other for the relationship to hold together. A very powerful attraction between two people is usually of this kind. Each falls under the spell of their partner because strongly undeveloped aspects of their own personality are strongly developed in the other person. The mutual attraction may be so magnetic that they cannot live without each other and find it impossible to part even when it is the only solution to conflict and violence, because each feels only half a person without the other. This is often the basis of the tragic love stories you read about in the newspapers.

> Madge, a business consultant, and Jim, a taxi driver, met on holiday. They fell for each other almost instantly and decided to live together but quickly found themselves having rows about each other's behaviour, Madge, a strong-minded decision-maker with a lot of energy, resented what she saw as Jim's laziness. He seemed to her to not want to make any decisions affecting their life together and did little but sit around when he was not at work.
>
> Jim, on the other hand, found Madge bossy and pushy. When she wasn't making decisions for both of them she seemed to be planning useful things for him to do. The rows got worse until, eventually, they had marriage guidance help through Jim's doctor. In fact they were so different from each other that they were hardly able to relate to each other at all an everyday domestic level until some months after they began talking things through. Madge's drive and strong-mindedness left her unable to relax and allow Jim responsibility – and simply let him be himself. Jim, though, had been taking no responsibility, making no decisions and doing nothing outside his job. To stay together they had to meet each other half way and both gradually began to change as a result.

Another aspect of their relationship worth mentioning is that Madge was acting as a 'parent' to Jim, in the way that Harry did for Kate, a sure way to create resentment sooner or later.

We find ourselves in these situations as adults because of the view we have of ourselves. It is easy to grow up adopting fixed values and ideas of who we are and it is only when these are challenged that we are likely to change. Marriage is one of the strongest challenges because, generally speaking, men and women react differently to change. Men generally do not learn how to go through changes because they do not have the same experience as women.

A girl changes to a woman as she reaches child-bearing age. If she marries she changes her name and then may become a mother. When her children grow up her role as a mother essentially disappears, then she must change again.

The woman tends to learn about change and, with her intuitive nature, she is emotionally more flexible than a man who may never change after reaching puberty. He may never even notice the changes she goes through. Instead, a man often remains static emotionally and does not grow and mature. This often results in the woman growing ahead emotionally and intellectually, leaving the man behind in the process to the point that she may literally leave because she can no longer relate to him. Men being outgrown by their wives will often use blocking tactics, not questioning why things have changed between them, nor wanting to find out about themselves or what is going on. Instead, they may blame the woman and other people around, or just switch off.

These differences take us back to the masculine–feminine polarities in both men and women discussed in the last section. A woman enters a relationship with expectations of masculine qualities while the man has feminine expectations of the woman. At the same time the inner feminine quality in the man reacts with the woman and the woman's inner masculine quality reacts with the man. This helps to affirm the sense of self in both of them. However, each communicates differently. Because she usually functions at an intuitive feeling level, the woman essentially expects the man to understand her without having to put her feelings into words. To her, many areas of life are implicit. But he is mystified by her behaviour because he needs things to be made explicit. He expects her to be logical and rational but she does not function only in that way. If they each cannot use their masculine and feminine qualities appropriately *on both sides* they will be at cross-purposes and clash.

It is only in relationships with the opposite sex that a balance of these qualities in each individual can be achieved. This begins in childhood in relationships with parents and other adults, then continues with living together or marriage when people become adult. If two people have not achieved a reasonable balance separately before living together or marrying then their differences may lead to a breakdown.

A further complication arises if, as sometimes happens, the energies of a particular couple are reversed so that the woman has more masculine energy than the man and the man is functioning mainly through his feminine energy. This was one of the problems facing Madge and Jim. It was very difficult for Madge to accept that she had a very strong personality compared with Jim and that he had gentle qualities which she was inclined to overlook and could learn from. Equally, it was hard for Jim not to feel emasculated by Madge and also to accept that there were aspects of masculine behaviour that he could learn from Madge.

The only way that the personality differences which couples meet can be dealt with constructively is for each to learn from the other. It takes a willingness to communicate, to share thoughts and feelings – even at the risk of appearing ridiculous. And it demands a willingness to learn something more about yourself.

Getting away from stereotypes

Every person is unique but part of the puzzle of that uniqueness, and therefore ourselves, is understanding who we are underneath the layers of conditioning by parents, school and the world at large. To be sure of and pleased with our true identity is the biggest step towards relating well to others and making partnerships which work.

Certainly this has a lot to with individuality, and some people clearly are more individualistic than others. Someone, for example, who has a strong, definite character can be seen to act in ways which mark them out as different from others despite the pressure to conform. But is this enough? How 'different' is being different and how 'conformist' is someone who conforms?

Let's take an example. Someone who has not conformed and has shown these characteristics through her individuality is the American actress Katharine Hepburn. Born in 1907, she was one of six children of a rich and progressive East Coast family which lived, however, in a community that was very conservative. A newspaper article, in describing her background, explained that the parents encouraged the children to express themselves and speak their minds from an early age.

Dr Hepburn (her father) believed in physical exercise as a life force and Katharine was doing acrobatics and swinging on trapeze as a child. At school she was an all-round athlete, as well as a swimmer, diver and even a figure skater. 'If there was a race, I always wanted to be first. I really was not brought up to feel that women were under-dogs. I was totally unaware that we were the second-rate sex' (*Sunday Times Magazine*, 7 February 1982).

Her early career in Hollywood was controversial, and the actress, who all her life has never suffered fools, frequently engaged in newsworthy battles with directors and producers.

Hepburn made her name with her very first film, *A Bill of Divorcement*, in 1932 and, says the article, George Cukor who directed it 'admired the way she brought her fine intelligence to the performance, triumphing over her inexperience in film technique'.

So, in her twenties, Miss Hepburn demonstrated many of the qualities that reveal a mature, well-adjusted person in charge of her own life. These qualities continued to be put to good use in a legendary film career and relationship with Spencer Tracy spanning decades during which, unlike many other stars, she kept her feet firmly on the ground. As the article notes: 'She has always cherished her privacy, keeping her home life as far away from her career as possible . . . Hard tussles with illness have not diminished her enthusiasm for energetic sports such as tennis and sailing and her conquering of Parkinson's disease is as much due to her ruggedness and singleminded refusal to be crippled as expert medical care.'

Katharine Hepburn is what the psychologist Abraham Maslow would call a self-actualising person: that is someone who is creative in the wide sense, has a vocation and is goal-oriented and able to maintain a productive relationship with others. Maslow maintains that some of the most-loved people in history displayed these characteristics and Miss Hepburn certainly has been loved. She is also, you will notice, very well in touch with the masculine principle of her psyche, that is she has a good deal of drive and ability to dictate events when she has a mind to.

Of course, you may say, it helps to come from a wealthy, progressive family, and that is true. It does confer advantages in life so that a person has a greater ease in succeeding in the world. But the 'active principles' which Miss Hepburn shows hold true for everyone. It's a matter of gaining access to them.

Maslow maintains that all self-actualising people achieve success in many areas of their lives though they don't necessarily become famous. What they are doing is becoming uniquely themselves.

Unconventionality itself isn't uniqueness. The trick is to reach those true qualities we all have but which, in many of us, are obscured or blocked as we grow up. Being different isn't enough because it is easy, then, to fall unawares into behaving in ways which merely react against conventionality and so exchange one form of behaviour for another.

To return to Jung briefly, we find that stereotyped behaviour, whether conventional or unconventional, can spring from psychological archetypes, so that what appears unconventional on the surface can be, more accurately, merely another kind of behaviour pattern. Marie-Louise von Franz, a collaborator of Jung's, devotes a whole book to one particular archetype, the *Puer Aeternus*. This is the eternal youth, someone in whom 'all those characteristics that are normal in a youth of 17 or 18 are continued in later life, coupled in most cases with a strong dependence on the mother'.

The eternal youth is the man who has not grown up and will try at almost any cost to avoid any responsibility as an adult. Accordingly, he is likely to go in and out of relationships, or not take marriage seriously, and be unable to cope with any kind of humdrum work. More explicitly, Marie-Louse von Franz says of him:

> The typical disturbances of a man who has an outstanding mother complex are, as Jung points out, homosexuality and Don Juanism . . . There is always the fear of being caught in a situation from which it may be impossible to slip out again. At the same time, there is something highly symbolic – namely, a fascination for dangerous sports, particularly flying and mountaineering – so as to get as high as possible, the symbolism of which is to get away from mother: that is from the earth, from ordinary life
>
> (von Franz, 1970).

We tend to see our personality in simple terms when we are really very complex with many different and contrasting facets of character.

The more we discover about ourselves, the more enriched and full our life can be. Many things in life can be seen as a way by which nature gives us feedback about ourselves and who we are. These include the work we do, exercise and sport, dance and theatre and the arts generally. Illness and religious practices have this meaning as do yoga and dreams properly interpreted. One of the great teachers is relationships with others; our need for them with all that it brings makes a constant comment on our uniqueness.

CHAPTER TWO

Changes in Marriage

The symbol for crisis in written Chinese is represented by the two-part character 'danger' and 'opportunity' – an apt description of some periods in any marriage. The top part of the character means 'closing down' which could be interpreted as not facing a situation and dealing with it; the bottom half means 'opening out', thus using the opportunity to develop as individuals.

Every close relationship we experience from the time we are born teaches us something about ourselves. The intimacy of marriage with its long-term commitment is a vehicle for personal change and the exchange of love. But where the marriage tie itself takes over from this process, then many of the influences to do with personal values, how to live and love and achieve our own potential, may be blocked. Marriage is essentially about both relating to another person and being yourself. In their book about assertiveness, *Don't Say Yes When You Want to Say No*, Herbert Fensterheim and Jean Baer put it this way:

> In the ideal close relationship, you establish a communion with another human being where feelings come first and you cannot separate giving and taking. In the optimal close relationship, the other person is like part of yourself. In fulfilling the other person's needs as if they were your own, you satisfy your own needs. Yet, you remain yourself as an individual. Thus both husband and wife are led to deeper, richer experiences and in the merging the individuality of each becomes stronger
>
> *(Fensterheim and Baer, 1976).*

Being able to state your own needs, and understand your partner's, is fundamental to close relationships. The quality of a particular marriage makes a clear comment on a couple's ability as individuals to relate and yet be themselves.

Most of us take into marriage a complex mixture of values, feelings, hopes and desires. They originate in our upbringing, in our education and in those ideas which we have absorbed from society at large, for example through television, newspapers and the people around us. Yet few of us can easily cope for long with a commitment of this kind at the age we choose to – usually in the twenties. Instead we carry into marriage a hotchpotch of feelings and ideas about how to live with someone and what we expect: love, happiness, security, status, the companionship found in a stable relationship and, for most of us, a partner with whom we feel committed enough to have children.

These powerful ideas which in some measure cater for important needs may, at the same time, cut across the unconscious yet vital needs of two individuals: the psychological and almost biological urge to change and develop throughout adult life. The maturing has to continue during a close relationship such as marriage; indeed it is a function of it, as we explained in the previous chapter on the dynamics of relationships. It is no wonder then that every age of marriage has its hazards.

The vital needs we are talking about, and which marriage ideally confirms, include having someone to love, acceptance of ourselves as we really are by our partners, reflection back of our uniqueness, and confirmation of our worth. Marriage has to include an awful lot and it is no wonder that marriages often do not last. It can be very difficult for partners to give to each other freely at this level if their responses are cluttered by inflexible ideas of what marriage is about, stemming from unhelpful personality traits and learned social attitudes. For example, couples who view marriage primarily as doing the right thing by society are likely to act in rigid and stereotyped ways which will become inadequate if either partner begins to change. This change for an individual can be particularly threatening when views of marriage are linked to strong cultural or religious ideas. The guilty feelings which are generated due to the conflict of emerging new attitudes and values in contrast to the old can be very destructive. They often lead, for example, to illness which, as we discuss in the chapter on Professionals, may be a symptom of a relationship in trouble. That many people's marriage problems can be seen to relate to strict doctrines of the various churches in society is becoming less relevant now with more flexible attitudes developing. It is to be remembered that although the churches are often perceived as authoritarian, rigid, or even irrelevant, there are many understanding people within them.

The marriage service contains promises of a lifetime's commitment and is also a public statement of this to the world. However, before this seal of approval is given the churches often don't discuss fully with couples what commitment they are really entering. How often do we see the spiritual world of the church and its values as irrelevant to the demands of everyday life – something which needs to be followed just for the 'day' and then forgotten about in our daily lives? As families we may encourage this ceremony (if we are totally honest with ourselves) to fill our need for the sense of occasion it provides and for 'doing the right thing'.

In close-knit religious families the sense of commitment is more likely to be carried through in everyday life. Yet the aim for all is marriage experienced in a deep and lasting way, in the true sense of caring deeply for another person as much as for ourselves.

Increased awareness of how old values and attitudes are linked to marriage breakdown has provoked a great deal of work in the last few decades by psychologists, marriage counsellors and feminists, leading to a revolution in the state of marriage. The divorce rates alone reveal how many people are experiencing these changes. They feel helpless as the emotions and ideals which have spurred them into marriage seem insufficient to sustain it, which makes them examine their personal values and seek a code by which to live. Couples are forced by circumstances to look at the underlying realities of their own marriage sooner or later, often to find that longstanding assumptions are contradicted.

The ways in which these assumptions handicap a relationship were spelled out in the early 1970s in a famous book, *Open Marriage*, by a husband and wife anthropological team, Nena and George O'Neill (1973). They crystallised the problem by showing that couples, and particularly conventional couples, tend to enter marriage by unconsciously creating a rigid framework of unwritten rules which governs their behaviour and subtly blocks their development as individuals. The O'Neills called this framework the Closed Marriage Contract and showed that these unwritten rules are clauses in the contract.

The clauses or conditions they listed are: possession and ownership of the mate; sacrificing one's individual identity; always acting as a couple; adopting rigid 'male' and 'female' roles and insisting on absolute fidelity by coercion. This tacit agreement, the O'Neills said, results in 'cutting you off not only from the outside world but from your natural desires'.

Despite the suggestion implied in the book's title, *Open Marriage* does not encourage irresponsible free-living relationships for every couple in which any married person should do as they please. Instead it shows ways in which people can live more fully and face some of the more intricate responsibilities of marriage and similar relationships. Paramount is the idea of true companionship and the willingness of both partners to give each other the emotional space to develop and be themselves.

Another key book of the last three decades which has influenced many people's attitudes to contemporary marriage is Betty Friedan's *The Feminine Mystique* (1965). Written shortly before *Open Marriage*, it revealed the emptiness of many women's lives in traditional marriages in the United States – and struck a powerful chord in Europe. It described husbands and wives both trapped within stereotyped male and female roles, their creativity stifled. The book showed that many women needed, as much as men, to make some mark in the outside world and that, by being brainwashed into staying in the kitchen by advertising and the society's attitudes, they had in effect been robbed of their talents and sense of identity. In *The Second Stage* (1982) Betty Friedan advocated a path that brings a new twist to the problem: that women need to find a way both to make their mark in the world *and* fulfil their needs as homemakers – in other words to integrate their masculine and feminine nature, and that men must do the same.

A great number of marriages in both Europe and the United States founder in the first few years. Why should this be? Feelings of disappointment and failure, coming after the many high hopes, are saying something fundamental about a couple's choice to marry or their ability to adapt to the demands of a close and committed relationship. Most of us assume – and indeed are encouraged to assume – that when we marry intimacy and a sense of 'one-ness' will solve all differences. In reality, though, marriage is a relationship requiring constant negotiation between two different people. In thriving relationships negotiation goes on all the time, often as much over small things such as doing household chores as over big issues. And a shared sense of humour helps to dispel niggling resentments. Each other's faults can be commented on, at the right moment, in ways that generate laughter rather than confrontation.

The issue of gender plays a key role in how a man and a woman communicate with each other. A good example is given by the counsellor Zelda West-Meads (1995), in describing how men and women approach a problem: 'Men need to learn to understand their partner's need to talk things through more, and to appreciate that, for her, talking is not just about sharing information and discussing solutions but also about feeling understood and supported.'

We tend to underestimate, or even disregard, such demands because we may not even be aware that they exist. Yet lacking maturity, knowledge and the behaviour skills necessary to live in an intimate relationship with someone may make it impossible for a couple to cross the important threshold from romantic love to meeting the challenges of day-to-day living.

Once we find that as well as virtues, our partner has common failings and irritating habits, we become disappointed. The image we have of them is flawed and their habits can take over in our imagination as the most important thing we see. It is at this point in any relationship – which may occur within a few weeks or some years – that the deeper relationship really begins; and here that two people, to live amicably together, need to take account of each other's sensitivities.

One person's habits such as, for example, dropping clothes on the floor, stubbing out a cigarette end on a plate, or not giving clear answers to questions, can quickly lead to disenchantment. Increasing resentment may build up an underlying atmosphere over a long period and, if these differences remain unchecked, communication may fail altogether. Rows, accusations, long silences and similar unhelpful behaviour which becomes habitual may also establish the beginnings of a breakdown in communication and sow the seed for divorce. The only way forward is to express the underlying feelings and objections so that some resolution can be found or accommodation made. By this we don't mean 'nagging' but honest discussion about respective needs in which each partner says how they feel.

Marriage demands adaptation and a fundamental change of behaviour for most people. A sticking point can arise from an unwillingness to make the emotional move from being a single person to sharing as a couple.

Having grown past this point of early change, which may cause little problem for many couples, marriage then requires that both partners explore themselves as a couple *and individually*. This is part of the process of continuous personal development we have talked about, and it provides the basis of intimate communication. Such intimacy goes far beyond the cosy togetherness and sexual success we are taught is the basis of marriage. As Nena and George O'Neill put it:

> *Love and cosiness, deeper emotional feelings, honest and open revelations, are seldom shared by husband and wife. By cutting themselves off from all possibilities of growth, they cut themselves off from their potential selves, and finally from one another*
>
> (*O'Neill, 1973*).

The most profound change during marriage is the birth of the first child. It changes everything. The balance of a couple's relationship alters irrevocably and they have to assume new roles for which emotionally it is almost impossible to prepare. Even the most competent people can flounder, but the effect on many marriages is devastating.

Most of all, this affects the woman. Vivienne Welburn (1980), in her book *Postnatal Depression*, points out that birth in a modern hospital, with a high-technology approach, effectively robs a mother of her control of an essentially creative act. Even worse, she is separated from her family, friends and other children and left to 'share the most private and personal of all experiences with strangers'. This lowers her self-esteem and can trigger depression. Although many men are now present at their children's birth, this cannot compensate for the experience a woman may have in such an impersonal system.

The full significance of being parents emerges when the baby is taken home. As Vivienne Welburn says: 'There is nothing in the traditional male role which helps a man to cope with the nurtur–ing his wife needs while she is nurturing their baby. Men expect to receive care, not give it.' She reports, for example, that few men notice if their wife is becoming depressed though they are in the best position to do so. If the depression continues and a pattern becomes established it can undermine the relationship.

Growing children make huge demands on their parents' time which makes it extremely difficult to find the time that they need to share with each other. An important aspect of being together is being apart, in the sense of allowing some time and space for themselves as individuals. This involves a need to do some activity purely for oneself and without the partner. Simple yet important ways in which many people do this include quietly reading in the same room as their partner, visiting friends alone or even taking a long, peaceful soak in the bath. More clear-cut ways include taking a regular class, or a separate holiday. Many men simply go fishing.

The failure to create one's own space can have serious consequences, particularly for women, as Jeannette Kupfermann (1981) says in *The MsTaken Body:* 'Depression as a bid for space and sanctuary has, as yet, gone unrecognised by psychiatrists . . . Do women innately recognise the need they have for periodic sanctuary to aid both physical and spiritual readjustment?'

The continuing pressures on women to run a home and family make it especially difficult for them to find this space, particularly during the childbearing years, while most men at least can quietly read the papers and many automatically follow an interest or hobby outside the home. Yet everybody has to have this space for their own well-being. As one psychologist points out, 'the need for privacy is universal' and that privacy is one of the hardest things to ask for without offering rejection (*Evening Standard*, 30 November 1982).

Couples have another significant need which has to be met if their relationship is to grow. This is time away from everyday pressures. The writer Erica Jong (1995) says, in *Fear of Fifty:* 'We also give our marriages too little space for pleasure. The result is that we flee from them, searching for ourselves. We think we have lost our souls. And we have. But we probably could find them together – if only we knew how.'

The commitment of marriage with the ties and natural restrictions that this involves forces many people to take a hard look at their situation sooner or later. In the late twenties and around the age of thirty we may feel a sense of unease. A person may be established in a career or comfortably married, often both, or perfectly happy to remain unattached, but in some way this may no longer be enough so that our certainties no longer sustain us. We may question our marriage or job, or perhaps find ourselves taking a lover. Circumstances can focus our attention in ways which show that we have been living with a false sense of security. A common fear of people in their late twenties is that life holds little for them after thirty and some single people suddenly marry about then, having felt increasingly that life was passing them by.

Dissatisfaction which builds up during the thirties may emerge as deep conflict at a time when a home is well established and children, if there are any, are probably at school. There is more scope for one or both partners to reflect on the differences between them. These can surface, for example, as boredom and a lack of spark in the relationship which may be drifting. One ex-husband said: 'Although we hardly ever went out, whenever I suggested that we did something interesting or different together, Jenny rarely responded. After a while I felt I was being blocked – as if a wall was being built up in front of me month by month.'

At this time too, personality differences which may not have mattered before can become polarised so that two people's needs feed each other in a destructive way, creating a pattern which will dominate their everyday life. For example, the over-helpful wife who waits on her idle husband, and the man who dominates every conversation while the woman is content to say little, may find in the end that each dislikes the other for it. What was an unconscious collusion at first develops into resentment and anger that the other partner is acting in that way when each needs to behave differently.

The age around forty to fifty is another period when many people feel unsettled in marriage and sometimes make sudden changes. Often dubbed the 'mid-life crisis' this is the realisation that the youthful years have gone and old age, as they see it, is all that lies ahead. This is why it is not unusual for men and women reaching their forties to become disillusioned with their life, or kick against a longstanding marriage by becoming involved with someone much younger.

A compelling urge for some people in their forties is to make a positive change and sometimes they may give up their job and embark on a completely new career or lifestyle. Sometimes a person realises that they need to make a complete re-evaluation deep within themselves and a big change can be part of carrying this out. Where a relationship needs to change and develop at this point, a couple can use the opportunity to work through these problems. In this way they can avoid burning too many boats and becoming victims of the situation.

However, the 'mid-life' crisis goes far deeper than simply changing partners, finding a new career or coping with the menopause. Everybody has an unconventional side somewhere in their nature. If that remains completely suppressed as an adult it can burst out in ways which cut across the values you hold at the time. This may be difficult to handle. We believe the middle years are not a stage you merely 'get through' but are more concerned with the process of maturing. It is at this time that the attitudes and experiences of the past gathered together shape the individual's attitude to the future. This can be a period of subtle changes in which, ideally, a more measured view is reached and wisdom grows.

The physical changes that occur in both sexes with ageing have to be acknowledged but the easy acceptance, for example, that poorer health is now 'normal' is, we believe, a way of giving up, an attitude of mind which interferes with the maturing process. Exercise, yoga and nutrition courses, among others, teach people to think about themselves and stay fit and youthful. This helps them remain physically and emotionally well and able to adapt as they grow older.

However, other people who have more fixed ideas about ageing often run into health and other problems which are reflected in the marriage relationship. These can be traced through to a lack of communication at a feeling level and also to one or both partners' difficulties in coming to terms with their identity – who they are now and what they want to do with the rest of their lives.

The middle and later years of marriage, when the children are usually striking out on their own, can be the richest for a couple who continue to relate closely. Their ability to change in step with each other makes drastic change, such as running off with a younger person, less necessary to their own development. Social norms are no longer necessarily keeping couples married in the later years when the situation for one or both is clearly deteriorating. Boredom and dissatisfaction are nowadays no less likely to lead to divorce in the fifties and beyond than at an earlier age.

As we have shown, one of the keys to a growing marriage is for each partner to be able to spend time apart from the other, for themselves, without feeling rejected. Until women collectively became more assertive, there was little recognition that they too need their own outlets. But this still leaves the problem of relating and true sharing to be resolved by each person, through understanding their own and their partner's needs.

CHAPTER THREE

Unhappy Marriage

Most long-term relationships fall into patterns of one kind or another. It is necessary to step back periodically to see if any changes need to be made to maintain a close understanding. For couples who divorce this hardly ever happens: instead, when things start to go wrong, closeness and intimacy may slip into off-handedness. Couples can become distant, argumentative or even violent. As time passes unresolved sources of friction assume more and more importance, or else a couple become passing strangers in their own home.

Feelings of boredom, tiredness and listlessness are among the first indications of marriage difficulties but they are subtle ones since they can equally indicate temporary fatigue or other problems, perhaps at work or elsewhere in the family.

Other danger signs indicating a restlessness with the relationship that suggest underlying disharmony may be signified by a change of habits in one or both partners. Things you have put up with may now become irritating so that even simple habits, like your partner leaving a mess in the bathroom, or carelessly slamming doors, become wearing and set you on edge. Or you find that you have gradually taken a dislike to your partner, for no apparent reason, and don't know how to deal with it. Or it may be that one of you increasingly gets home late, or works away from home more often so that the normal pattern of relating slips away.

The sense of disappointment that this generates brings many people up short. Feelings of dismay, puzzlement and even anger may intrude upon your thoughts while you go about your daily tasks – at home, at work or while you relax. These feelings may affect you for some time before you realise it.

A wife of fifteen years said: 'When things changed between us it reached the point when I would drive home and sit outside in the car for half an hour before I could bring myself to go into the house.' Every circumstance of this kind, if unchecked, may lead to irreversible breakdown. Feelings may be disjointed so that the situation becomes confused and uneasy and you may feel puzzled at something in the atmosphere which you probably ignore or try to shrug off at first. Gradually these feelings keep returning until you cannot ignore them, and you are likely then to try to understand what is happening. It may be that you begin noticing things which are wrong in other people's marriages and start making comparisons with your own. Some people compare notes with close friends, though this is more common among women who, as a matter of course, spend more time discussing their personal lives with each other than men do.

On the other hand divorce for some gradually becomes a reality after years of argument or other difficult behaviour such as heavy drinking, violence, gambling or persistent affairs. It may be a very long time before someone realises and accepts the hopelessness of situations like these and then suddenly they resolve to take the first steps towards divorce. This new attitude may also show in the sentiment that 'they are no longer the person I married' or 'I am no longer the person my partner married'.

The build-up of all these feelings may occur over years when a difficult or unpleasant marriage is accepted as normal, yet they finally crystallise into the realisation that 'marriage is not supposed to be like this'. We may not have voiced directly what we want because we might be rejected, or this might involve change.

Two common ideas are paramount for most people here: that they have made a mistake by marrying the wrong person and the belief that they have failed.

The break-up of a marriage and family is a failure in simple terms but beyond this may be deeper contributing factors which could have been working away for a very long time – even from the beginning. Often a person will gradually realise that the feelings of closeness with their partner were only a mirage; that there was a lack of true relationship and real feelings were not exchanged. In *Don't Say Yes When You Want To Say No*, Fensterheim and Baer point out that

> *Many husbands and wives fail to achieve closeness in marriage because they hide behind the iron curtain of their public selves, and don't disclose their true feelings. They also, in ways both obvious and subtle,*

make it difficult for their partners to be open, getting upset when their partners speak freely and combating openness with verbal hits and hurts, or simply withdrawing from it into a closed shell. This sets up a joint spiral of increasing falseness

(Fensterheim and Baer, 1976)

There are marriages whose serious differences can be settled and a new understanding reached; where to break up would be to throw away too much that is worthwhile. The journalist Katherine Whitehorn says that a common misunderstanding is: 'If things get bad, they'll never get better again; as if the relationship were a flame that had blown out, not a fire that might need stoking.' Flexible attitudes make for successful marriages and, as Ms Whitehorn adds: 'Any number of variations are possible – but only if people have the guts and courage to stick with the situation and re-negotiate the contract if necessary' (*Good Housekeeping*, November 1982).

It is simple to begin divorce proceedings impulsively and the more people divorce, the more other couples may see divorce as the solution to their problems. And yet there must be many marriages that are essentially worthwhile and could be successful if the problems were worked through. It often happens, though, we believe, that even if a marriage has been successful, it reaches a point where it cannot continue if the two people involved are to develop as individuals and live fulfilling lives.

One person will usually recognise first that, as a couple, they have grown apart and feel that *their own* needs have changed. Because this does not deny that the marriage has been successful up to that point, it may be very hard for the other person to understand the nature of this change. The task for both is to clarify the extent of the rift and how it might be resolved. It may require professional counselling to understand the difficulties and find out whether they can be overcome.

The enormous strains of bringing up children test the parents' ability to adapt. No longer only a couple, the two partners have to try to maintain their own relationship while coping with the disruption and sheer hard work that accompany the joys of bringing up children. A wife becomes a mother and the husband a father, roles which produce unwritten rules of behaviour that subtly create a divide between them. If they fail to integrate these roles into their own relationship, then the image of parenthood takes over their ability to relate as individuals. Once identities become submerged in this way, the seeds of divorce may be planted. The ways in which women in particular become trapped in this pattern have been well documented, in particular by Betty Friedan (1965) in *The Feminine Mystique*, but some men also can be pulled in two, at equal cost. One husband said: 'Once our child was born I put all my energy into being "the good father" and doing "all the right things" until, in the end, the close relationship between Liz and me disappeared.'

With basically no preparation for marriage, the pressures of having babies and bringing up young children can result in personality changes which render a couple divorce-prone. The amount of work needed to run a home and family, which falls mostly on women, can be exhausting. As one businesswoman pointed out: 'By trying to combine the traditional roles of parent and homemaker with the demands of their paid work, many subject themselves to overload and stress' (Shirley, 1995). These demands in marriage are usually a heavier burden than can be anticipated and very difficult to deal with once they are there.

Men come under heavy pressure too. They very often have to live in two worlds – their daily work and family life in the home they come back to each day. Some have work which forces them to be away from home. If a man has uncertain employment, whether self-employed or on short contracts, or becomes unemployed, this puts strains on the marriage. Most men don't identify as strongly with the home as women – even women who have jobs outside the home – yet they are still usually providing the family's major income. This, combined with a sense of being neglected by their wives compared with the wives' attitude to them before the children came along, can lead to feelings of being wanted only as a provider.

Men have the characteristic of being able to be single-minded to the point where they can exclude other things going on which they ought to be attending to. This is how men achieve results in what they do whether at work or in a hobby. But this is hard for a woman to accept since she is forced by necessity to divide her capacity for single-mindedness among conflicting priorities. Though a man will concentrate for hours on his DIY or hobbies while the children get up to mischief and the refuse has not been put out, a woman will be concentrating on several things at once – perhaps studying for an exam while keeping an eye on the cooking and listening out for the children. Her ability to do these things at the same time leads to resentment that her husband simply concentrates on one thing and ignores everything else. Behind this is a fundamental difference in approach to life between the majority of men and women.

In a family in particular a woman with a strong, feeling nature does most of the caring. She may complain about her husband's lack of feelings yet have missed the opportunity that the relationship provides to teach him about this area of life and show how he might express it for himself. Of course, this pattern has deep roots going back to childhood upbringing and beyond. This is now an area which is rightly the concern of many feminists, but feminism has also shown that single-mindedness is necessary for women as well as men.

More hidden are the ambivalent feelings that many men and, increasingly, women have about being parents. No longer receiving the same attention as before, they often come to feel that marriage is more a series of demands than a state of love and companionship. To add to the point made by the businesswoman quoted, the total amount of work and pressures on wives (and husbands too) created by having children is, for many, a huge burden. Add to this the financial pressures many families face, and possibly the need to give constant care to a family member who is chronically ill or disabled, and it is no wonder that many marriages crumble. Yet some families, somehow, cope with seemingly overwhelming difficulties which cannot break the bonds that hold them together.

In almost every marriage the partners are expected to involve themselves with each other's relatives. The benefits can be enormous but, equally, in some families demands and personality differences intrude into a relationship so severely that they may undermine it. For example, constant interference from a parent or parents of one of the partners can leave the couple no space in which to create a life of their own – which leads to resentment. Lucy told us: 'For years Les and I more or less *had* to take holidays in his father's seaside bungalow in Devon. His father was a very forceful person and Les always felt obliged to go – and I went along with this until I could stand it no more. It was one of the reasons why we split up.'

Having a child is one way in which some couples consciously try to save their relationship in the mistaken belief that this will draw them together. It may be their first child or a further child after they have had a family. The likelihood is that to have a baby in these circumstances will not make the underlying problems go away, indeed it can make things worse and even precipitate breakdown. In any case a child can rarely provide the glue to hold together a drifting relationship.

A cooling of the normal and established sexual relationship is an obvious sign of a troubled marriage. Fatigue and depression can run even a healthy sexual relationship into difficulties but where a couple's sex life simply declines to a low level it is likely to be linked to other things. For example, unresolved sexual and communication problems may have become a part of the marriage. A marriage which falls into set habits, including sexual ones, can become boring and disillusion will set in. We tend to expect, for example, that sex will stay at the same intensity and are disappointed if it doesn't happen this way. Equally, we have various demands about sex which may not be realised as the relationship develops. Sex, at its best, is an intensely personal experience. In the context of marriage pressures it may be very difficult for two people to accept and go along with the unique sex life each relationship creates. If we cannot adapt and explore the subtleties which occur we may feel incomplete. More starkly, these differences, if unresolved, could amount to incompatibility. It could be that your partner is struggling with their sexual identity or an attraction for the same sex, and may have been throughout the marriage. Perhaps only now earlier subtle signs start to make sense. If the situation is now made overt, through an admission being made or direct confrontation, this is a crisis point that can lead to some solutions in spite of the confusing feelings you both may have.

You may need both factual information and to work through your feelings on this sensitive issue with a third party such as a doctor or counsellor. There can be a release which enables you to talk about your relationship as it really is.

A regular sexual relationship with one partner touches deep aspects of your personality. Success and difficulties in this area go back to childhood and adolescence, and the development of identity and self-esteem. Problems of communication in the relationship may be at their most acute when reflected in sex. A good example is 'having to perform' when one person falls into a pattern of acting in a way their partner expects, or believes they expect, or where two people's needs from sex are very different. Like marriage itself, a healthy sexual relationship depends on a commitment which is continually renewed.

Having children often affects a marriage so profoundly that a couple's sexual life may never be the same again. The changes and pressures once they start a family may prevent them from resuming their normal sexual relationship. But, as we said earlier, these problems, like post-natal depression, can indicate serious unresolved differences between them.

Finally, sexual cooling may be reflected in one partner taking a lover. That person may be reacting to a feeling of rejection by and/ or distance from their partner. Or they may look outside marriage for more stimulating company as well as better sex. The other partner may collude with this or not, or may be unaware of the change, but either way the emotional gap which has appeared is at risk of widening to a gulf where divorce is likely.

When a relationship is in trouble, for whatever reason, changes are taking place; and the knowledge that change is occurring is the essential first step to working with it. It may be months, even years, before one or both partners becomes aware of what is really happening because habits of everyday life act as a mask. The writer Monica Furlong (1981) explained that in spite of having a career, the support of a husband, and children, she felt 'something was very wrong'. She and her husband reached an impasse. 'I found myself very envious of friends of my own age who were not tied by marriage, all of whom seemed to be growing and learning to understand themselves in a way that I did not.'

When this realisation happens, it may trigger feelings of insecurity – emotional or financial – sadness, anger, rage and a whole range of unfamiliar emotions. A feeling of 'it can't be happening to me' is common, mixed with a heavy sense of inevitability which at first is usually pushed away. But it is important now to accept the reality of what is happening. This marks a further change in the atmosphere and the partner who knows may become visibly upset. They may become sullen or burst into tears yet deny, when questioned, that anything is wrong. It is at this point you must admit the problem and talk about it. This first step to talking takes courage. It may be the hardest thing to do because it is so painful to admit, even to yourself, and it is hard to know how your partner will react. Knowing that it will be painful to raise the subject and equally painful for your partner to hear, you may keep things to yourself for some time then find yourself confiding initially in a friend or relative.

> Bill said: 'I held my feelings in for so long that, finally, they burst out one day while I was talking to my sister-in-law. She seemed to know and was surprisingly sympathetic.'
> In Jackie's case her mother asked her point blank if she still loved Alan. 'I told her I didn't and that was the first time that I admitted the situation to anyone else.'

It is essential, now that the subject is exposed, that you do tell your partner your feelings. This is because you must accept the responsibility of dealing with the situation and also because you would simply be loading a third person with the burden of the secret. You can postpone the pain by not talking to your partner now but this leaves a burden with the person you have told.

The release of tension when the subject is brought into the open, with all its upsets and difficulties, makes a starting point. It is an opportunity for both partners to accept what is happening and begin to explore ways of coping. The mixed feelings involved, particularly failure and guilt, are hard to deal with – even frightening. It is hard to be rational and it may be some time before you and your partner can talk together constructively, if at all. What is now occurring is unique to each couple: a course of events with its own momentum which may last for a long time. Relationship breakdown has its own energy and is a process which has to be worked with.

The admission and acceptance we have talked about are a crucial stage in reaching the right state of mind to have some control over what follows in the months ahead. To face the issues and not shirk them is painful and in the short term an option which seems unnecessary, even masochistic. If you are actively considering divorce you might think, why talk about these things when it must surely be better to get the whole business over with as quickly as possible? Our answer is this: the pain is part of the healing process which will help you resolve doubts about yourself and guilt should you break up, and which will channel deep anger into necessary outlets. In the longer term, you may regret that you did not try to confront these factors now. Do you *really* know what your partner wants?

It takes time to develop a positive approach but to recognise this as the goal at this stage affects the course of your future life. The support and dependence on which you have relied in marriage has to alter, leaving you to re-establish or establish for the first time a sense of true independence. You will need this independence to establish a new pattern within the relationship whether staying together or not. This is partly because there will be an adjustment in the balance of emotional dependence between any two partners, and partly because habits, and ways in which they spend their time, will also undergo a change. This is a time to find inner strength to help discover what you will want in life in the future. It is very much a test of your identity – which demands that you examine who or what you really are or want to be.

To make these statements while still living with your partner can require considerable patience and skill; the situation may be tense, explosive or apathetic. The important thing is to work to dissolve communication blocks so that they do not become permanent. Sometimes it takes space, even separation, before two people can talk about their differences. Commonly all that happens is that one partner leaves and the other has to cope alone. Once living apart it is even harder to give the time to talk which is needed – a lot may depend on what can be resolved while you are still together. Longstanding disagreements may come to a head at this time or arguments arise from the issues. The way that you tackle these differences is a key to your relationship in the future – whether you stay together or not.

An unhappy marriage exposes underlying factors in both partners' emotional makeup. This is why the experience of breakdown is such a harrowing one. Arguments in this context are an expression of undeveloped areas of the personality, so that breakdown is one of the life crises during which a person is confronted with this (often irrational) side of their nature. The opportunity is offered to acknowledge that by altering your attitude you can deal more effectively with the immediate problems.

There are two kinds of arguments: constructive ones and destructive ones. We aim to show here how destructive tactics or slanging matches simply wreck the chances of reaching any progressive agreement. It is here that communication can stop permanently, leading to the familiar and expensive trail of bitter disputes, long talks with solicitors, court battles, fights over children and money – and resulting in the lifetime silence of the partner who refuses any further contact. This is the stuff of marital disputes which fills the newspaper columns. Constructive ways of dealing with disputes and putting your point of view will minimise these upsets, establish understanding and enable you to solve the inevitable problems of marriage break-up.

The biggest single obstacle to getting anywhere in arguments is *not listening*. Continual arguments that get no further than the superficial issues masking the real ones, or repeated exchanges of insults, produce a stalemate because feelings get in the way. Many people are simply unaware of the strength of their underlying feelings when they argue and it is essential to get in touch with these feelings before anything can change. Often this pattern of response has originated in childhood and now colours their reactions as adults to any kind of dispute. Often disputes literally trigger sensitive areas which release feelings of insecurity, fear and anger which are otherwise dormant, so a partner behaves as if they were a completely different person. When arguments go round in circles, become heated, or erupt uncontrollably month after month, they can reach the state described by Monica Furlong (1981):

> 'If *every* row feels like a life-and-death struggle, if living with someone evokes the huge emotions – terror, jealousy, envy, possessiveness, death-dealing rage – which normally we associate with grand opera or Shakespearean tragedy – then the situation may not be a livable one.'

To get anywhere there is a need to move beyond the shouting match and begin to argue constructively.

However, it is important to realise that any argument is an *interaction* between two people. They may have fallen out over a particular issue: an affair may be uncovered, or they may start an open discussion of their differences. Couples who continually argue or bicker are locked in a pattern both sides are perpetuating, even if one partner makes most of the noise. It is important to listen actively now to what the other person is really saying. Arguments may be confused and slide off the point, or go round in circles.

Often the real subject of the argument may not be raised, but somewhere within the dispute is the true issue. If you cannot find this issue and begin to deal with it then the help of a third party may enable a way forward to be found. Many people find a friend to confide in whose opinions they trust. Often such a person can provide some insights which may not have been considered before. But do not expect too much since a person who takes your side and merely backs up your opinions is not being really helpful. The friend who can listen without taking sides comes closer to the help you need, and may enable you to see the situation in a new perspective. These people are fairly rare but anyone who is helped in this way is very fortunate.

> Roger, who moved into Jim's flat after an explosive row with
> Miriam, said: 'I was very lucky. Jim was incredibly patient while
> I poured out my troubles. Though he did no more than listen, it
> helped me find the patience to go back and start to talk things
> through.'

Some people spend their whole lives reacting to even trivial difficulties in an argumentative manner – in and outside marriage. Some argue only with their partners and show only their 'good side' to the outside world, and again this is a pattern between partners. If you are married to someone who is like this, you are dealing with a non-listener *par excellence*, someone who cannot hear what the other person is saying because they usually get too wound up to separate the issues from their own internal anger. If your partner is like this in marriage, a break-up is usually stormy, traumatic and needs special handling to break the pattern because this kind of person feeds on continuing argument.

Take note if you are inclined to be like this yourself. The first rule is to try progressively to avoid getting drawn into more arguments. By not shouting back or making pointed comments you stop fuelling the urge in yourself to argue. The aim is to talk firmly and calmly, making essential points while knowing the direction you want the discussion to follow. If you feel you are getting no further, it is sensible to close the subject until another time. You can say, for example: 'I can't talk any more about this now,' or, 'I need a break, let's discuss it tomorrow.' It takes courage and persistence to adopt this approach, together with time, considerable patience and acceptance of your own part in the problem. It may be months before there are noticeable changes but by sticking to it you take charge of the situation and gain some control over it, as we have said before. By refusing to provide the feedback that fuels the arguments, the climate can change, and the pattern will alter. In the calmer atmosphere that follows you can talk rationally for at least part of the time and find common ground.

A major difficulty when two people are in disagreement can be their different ways of seeing and dealing with problems. This stems from our individual psychological make-up. Men's strengths are often the logical rational function of the mind – the capacities to calculate, invent, build and look at things from an objective point of view which are governed by the left hemisphere of the brain. On the other hand women's strengths are often the feeling, intuitive functions of the mind – empathy, artistic senses and non-logical thought processes governed by the brain's right hemisphere. These are different ways of knowing and of expressing ourselves which are balanced to a different degree in each individual and both are equally valid.

Where a person is dominated by one of these functions with the other undeveloped – as occurs in either sex – they may find it difficult to cope in situations where the undeveloped function should come into play. This can often be seen where a couple argues constantly without ever reaching any solutions. Each person is effectively talking a different language. More fortunate are those people whose rational and intuitive sides are equally developed for they can understand and relate more fully to a partner, and so deal with disagreements in a balanced way. Two people who function in this way can solve their differences far more constructively than those who cannot begin to understand each other's point of view. Communication can break down as a result of not recognising the other areas of the argument. It can also be seen in situations where a couple will not discuss their problems, and continue as if nothing is happening. Or it may be that one person realises that something is wrong but cannot get a response from their partner who refuses to acknowledge that there are difficulties. This behaviour often produces the classic outcome where one partner suddenly leaves a marriage 'without any warning' and the person left behind is totally mystified, having never realised anything was wrong.

Other barriers to effective communication are sarcasm, stubbornness and pride. Sarcastic comments are never helpful but merely express buried anger that twists the knife in any argument. More than this, sarcasm undermines the chances of reaching agreement or even the trust which must be the basis of any agreement. Similarly, persistent stubbornness shows a lack of willingness to meet the other person half way, and this is often at the root of those break-ups which remain stuck in inflexible attitudes and lead to miserable and drawn out divorces. The positive side of stubbornness is that you may need to stick to your principles on some particular issue such as the welfare of the children, but beware if you continue to hold a fixed attitude on every issue. Stubbornness is strongly linked to excessive pride, where deep down a person feels that their identity is threatened if they concede anything in dispute to the other person. It is worth remembering that in a marriage argument, as in any other, the person you argue with is usually right some of the time.

Not everyone has the communication skills which enable the normal problems in marriage to be resolved. These include being sensitive to others' feelings and realising the effect that words have on other people. Family patterns of upbringing have an important bearing on this. Families in which, for example, little opportunity for discussion is created, or where it is normal to say hurtful things to each other, do not foster the art of saying what you mean in a constructive way. In contrast, the skills needed to communicate properly are deliberately taught in the fields of industrial relations and business management, where the havoc that is caused by the lack of them is well recognised.

Some people instinctively have these abilities and it comes naturally to them to use a very definite technique when talking to others. For example, they will wait for a response after making a point in an argument, which allows the other person to take in what has been said and make a reply. This may also show that the listener did not understand the point that was made and it might have to be clarified or explained in a different way. You can act similarly by listening and responding carefully. If you are receiving mainly abuse, it is usually better to ignore it and keep to the issue at hand or end the conversation until a better time.

The constructive use of silence during a discussion of differences provides two things. If you wait before replying after something is said, it shows the other person that you are prepared to listen to their view. It also lowers the temperature because you are less likely to blurt out unconsidered remarks which inflame the situation.

A second way is to try to be non-judgemental. This involves not rejecting out of hand what your partner may say. To disagree constantly will put them on the defensive and make them angry. To continue in this way arouses recriminations, blocks progress and suppresses the real issues. The aim is for each to allow the other person to say what they feel and move on progressively from there.

Finally, honesty is the thread which enables a discussion to move towards a conclusion, at least an interim one. Honesty means showing your true feelings so that your partner knows exactly how you feel. Honest anger is better than veiled insults and can clear the air even though this may be upsetting. Honesty also means that you should not hide any information from your partner that they ought to know. For example, if you have a lover you want to leave for, it is confusing and unfair to hide this to avoid the repercussions and a mistaken kindness to believe you are sparing the other person's feelings by doing so. It is only when you are honest that the real issues can be openly discussed.

Constant arguments in the presence of children, or unresolved tension between their parents in the home, undermines children's emotional development and peace of mind. Parents and family are a very large part of a child's world and parents' unhappiness is often reflected in changes in their children's behaviour. These include temper tantrums, changed eating and sleeping patterns, difficulties at school and regression to an earlier phase of childhood. Serious and fundamental differences between adults should not be a part of the child's world – because children 'pick things up' – and should be dealt with in privacy. In this way children are not pressured by the adult world they are too young to cope with.

Children's needs are often forgotten or ignored by parents who are too absorbed in their own problems. We talk more fully in a later chapter about how children can be helped when a relationship is in trouble, but it is worth mentioning here that once a couple begin to resolve the issues between them children's difficulties also begin to ease.

The psychologist Frances Wickes quotes a case of a disturbed girl aged about nine who was affected by her parents' cold relationship. They chose eventually to part and the girl's behaviour became normal again. As Frances Wickes (1977) says, she was 'a victim of the wrong atmosphere in the home, and her trouble disappeared as soon as her parents settled theirs'.

Illness as a symptom of an unhappy marriage can be found in both adults and children. In adults this is expressed in many forms, some obvious and some more subtle, so that the person affected may make no connection between events in their life and what is happening to their body or mind. The widespread dependence of many thousands of women worldwide on tranquillisers and antidepressants (psychotropic drugs) as they look after their husbands and families is a case in point. They are prescribed by doctors because of women's difficulty in coping with the special pressures in their everyday lives. Many of these women are seriously burdened, as the sociologist Ann Oakley says, 'with too much to do plus the demands of a husband' (*Observer*, 20 January 1980). Yet there are others who do not have these burdens but lead leisured, well-ordered lives in expensive homes. Such women too are on tranquillisers in large numbers; so these problems are not specific to marriage itself but are reflections of a relationship or lifestyle which does not meet their inner needs.

What can be the cause of an illness which affects people from such different backgrounds in the same way and requires strong medication to cope with it? We find ourselves looking again through *The Feminine Mystique* and Betty Friedan's descriptions of 'the problem with no name'. She identifies the difficulty facing almost every wife in one succinct sentence: 'It is easier to live through someone else than to become complete yourself.' We agree with her that this need for identity cannot be ignored, and that the question she posed in the 1960s 'Who am I?' is still fundamental to everyone and not just to women. We believe that the failure of many women to ask that question and take responsibility for their lives exacts a heavy price.

An increasing number of doctors are sure that many physical and mental illnesses cannot be divided from the psyche. When a person is under stress in an unhappy marriage we believe that there is a whole spectrum of illnesses to which partners of either sex may fall victim. An American psychiatrist, Wayne Dyer (1977), in a book on personality problems, says: 'There is a burgeoning amount of evidence to support the notion that people even choose things like tumours, influenza, arthritis, heart disease, "accidents" and many other infirmities, including cancer, which have always been considered something that just happens to people.'

The list of illnesses which fall into the category of psychosomatic diseases is elastic and at the present time partly speculative. For example, migraine and many skin conditions are widely accepted as psychosomatic in origin but no one can be sure yet to what extent heart disease, kidney disease and cancer follow the same pattern. However, a growing number of doctors are certain that these diseases have their origins in difficult and stressful situations in life, of which a collapsing marriage is one. As we said in our first chapter, the body, mind and emotions need to work together in harmony if a person is to maintain good health. Sometimes it is only when these deep areas are explored that the link between them can be grasped. This self-exploration can bring benefits at a number of levels, as the experience of one person shows:

> Mark, a successful businessman, was unhappy at home and suffered from arthritis in his hands and migraine. Finally he found his way to a psychologist. Over a period of time she showed him that he was feeding his mind through his work but was unable to share his feelings in his marriage. The results of this imbalance were reflected in his physical condition. However, when he learned to get in touch with his feelings and show his wife more affection, his migraines and arthritis also eased.

People are not generally aware of the range of outside help that is available for those in marriage difficulties. In particular, we are talking about counselling and psychotherapy, in which, either alone or with a partner, different ways of dealing with the problems may be found. This is usually done at meetings, normally lasting an hour, over varying periods of time.

Radio phone-in programmes which deal with listeners' personal problems are a form of counselling – a two-way conversation mixed with advice which begins to make each problem more manageable. We talk about the various kinds of help available in greater detail in the chapter on Professionals.

Many couples never think of taking this course, others flatly refuse to try it when the idea is suggested, and it is common to leave it so late to seek this kind of help that divorce is almost inevitable. Most people feel it is a brave step to talk to a stranger about their personal problems, but the insights and clarity which a trained professional offers can, with time and patience, shed completly new light on a difficult situation. What is needed is to close the gap between expectations of marriage and the reality. A person's role and their needs in a relationship may be two different things.

CHAPTER FOUR

The Meaning of Affairs

One way in which some people seek independence and a sense of identity is by having an affair or a series of affairs. This need, perhaps for exploration, was identified in the headline in a newspaper article on the subject which said: 'Time and again people say an affair made them feel alive. It made them feel their lives were worthwhile'. Dissatisfactions and disappointments with marriage were shown to be the main reason why people chose to have affairs. But in a revealing paragraph a woman described how, when she was 'desperate and weary of life she decided against adultery and took a university course instead' her husband behaved exactly as if she was having an affair. She lied to get money for books and then read them in the bathroom.

This episode gives a clue to the complex underlying reasons behind affairs and, equally, suggests that an affair can be a crisis that has significantly deeper aspects than is generally realised. It is bound up with an individual's change and development.

The sense of something missing in marriage is a common one which people deal with differently. This tension was expressed in a special report on infidelity in a British newspaper, which said: 'The passion that we feel for the new, for the unknown, has little in common with the settled affection people feel for each other in a lengthy relationship. This kind of love . . . allows little scope for unpredictability and the shifting power relationships that are the spice of affairs' (*Guardian*, Infidelity – Special Report, 11–12 September 1995). Busy professional people can find, after a while, their individual activities are more absorbing than sharing life with someone else.

Research in the UK by the sociologist Annette Lawson (1995) has shown that about half of married couples experience infidelity, while therapists at the Tavistock Institute of Marital Studies, in London, found 'an affair is by far the most common presenting problem, often being the precipitating factor among couples who have been unhappy for some time to seek help' (Lawson, 1995). But, as the divorce lawyer Blanche Lucas put it, people expect too much from marriage anyway. Talking about the number of people who divorce in Britain, she said: 'The fantasies they have about marriage lead one to suspect that there has been something unrealistic about their upbringing: they think they are going to live happily ever after; they expect complete rapport at every level; a perfect sex life – whatever that may be' (*Observer*, 28 February 1982).

It is no wonder, given the variety of reasons why marriage and live-in relationships can pall, that people seek sexual companionship elsewhere. The search for romance and excitement is universal and in people who are truly alive lasts throughout life. The lives of many are made interesting by the exhilaration of a challenging job, an engrossing sport, by other highly creative leisure activities in the arts, or by travel. Having an affair can fulfil a similar need but it can also fulfil deeper ones relating to every person's need for affection, for being valued and for being accepted for oneself. More important, these qualities confirm our individual identity at the most intimate levels and lack of them, especially in marriage, amounts to deprivation. It is intimacy which provides this exchange but one which most individuals expect to include a number of different qualities – the emotional links of close sexual relationships. These links are suggested in the diagram:

Lover

Friend   Companion

When we marry we marry a lover. We also want a true friend and the nurturing and acceptance that companionship brings. When all these qualities are functioning together the relationship takes on a spiritual quality in the broadest sense. Often, though, they are not all there in the first place or else become lost or submerged as marriage slips into routine. To seek a lover is to admit (even if unconsciously) that one or more of these elements is missing in the marriage, and to look for them in another person. Some people do achieve a balance of what they want by finding it in two or more relationships but more usually a person will try to find in a lover all that they wanted from marriage but lost, or perhaps never had. At their most acute, these feelings are behind the action of lovers who dramatically run off together, yet this illusion is putting the same unrealistically high demands on the new relationship as on the old one. This is the reason why so many affairs run their wayward course only to end in unhappiness.

The risks and furtiveness which affairs involve reveal another underlying reason why people embark on them. Enjoyment of the secrecy and intrigue that is involved seems to provide its own *raison d'être* in many cases. The thrill of meeting and having sex with someone unknown to your partner, and perhaps to theirs too, provides a level of excitement which may not be present in a person's everyday life. There are people who, by nature, need to test themselves and take risks throughout their lives and to whom an affair is a part of expressing this urge. As women become more assertive and achieve greater economic independence, the emotional balance in marriage is being tipped. As a newspaper article expressed it, some 'career women are now sexual predators for sex, money and power, just as men have been traditionally.' Some researchers have concluded that being totally faithful in marriage is an ideal. The psychiatrist Julian Hafner (1993) says: 'Almost all of us expect our marriage partners to be sexually faithful, and most of us struggle to be faithful ourselves. Biologically, this is an absurd situation.' But persistent affairs suggest a continuing adolescence and behaviour which is unconscious even to the extent that a person never takes real risks of any sort in their everyday life. By refusing to grow up they are diverting creative energy which could be used more productively.

Another issue is the risk of infection which today is made more acute by the spread of the HIV virus leading to acquired immune deficiency syndrome (AIDS).

In her book *Putting It All Together*, the American psychologist Irene Kassorla relates extra-marital affairs to the notions taught during childhood that sex is dirty. The result, she says, is adults who seek illicit sex because they cannot enjoy open sex with their partners.

Extra-marital sex can keep the man a little boy or the woman a little girl. Lying, stealing, cheating, hiding from Mommy or Daddy is what little boys and girls do. People who are cheating on their mates are duplicating these childhood behaviours. The married man or woman who is promiscuous may still be hanging on to early childhood behaviour

(Kassorla, 1973).

Dr Kassorla says affairs can also be understood as a prime vehicle for anger and 'used as a substitute for anger when one partner is furious and can't express the anger directly'. Instead of standing up to the partner over some issue, a person will get their own back by having sex with someone else.

But the affair is like a smokescreen. It creates distance and keeps you from seeing what is really happening within your marriage. You're so happy with your lover that you become blind to your *role in the pain of your marriage. It prevents you from looking at* your *part in the problem*

(Kassorla, 1973).

This brings us to the idea of taking responsibility. Since affairs are normally an outward sign of marriages in trouble, there is an obligation sooner or later to look at the circumstances you find yourself in rather than be carried along. It is a question of taking control of your life and working through the problem areas. When we fail to do this our family life, work and our whole lifestyle may crumble.

Tony, a partner in a busy architect's practice, and Sheila, one of the secretaries, fell passionately in love and they began taking long lunch hours together. After a few weeks they were spending every available minute in each other's company and their work suffered to the extent of hardly being done at all. For some time their colleagues filled a lot of the gaps but eventually they became angry at the heavy work load. Finally, the other partners could no longer overlook Tony's inability to do his job and he was forced to take a less responsible job in another part of the building. Soon afterwards the affair petered into stalemate, his career lay shattered and he was left with the long haul to put the pieces back together at home.

Women frequently find themselves trapped in the position of falling in love with men who are not really free and some repeat the pattern again and again. In America an association, Other Woman's Forum, was formed some years ago to counsel women having affairs with married men. The main problem, a newspaper article explained, was the inevitable unhappiness which stems from falling in love with a man who usually remains securely married. As one woman put it: 'When he fails to get in touch for days or weeks – as he will when there is pressure of work or a risk of detection – then I sit in abject misery, getting bitter, feeling vindictive about the casual treatment I am getting; but there is no one to vent those feelings on.' This tortured waiting for the phone to ring is a picture of a typical *teenager* in love.

Surprisingly, the Forum's object was to strengthen the position of 'The Other Woman' by telling her that she cannot help falling in love and that she need feel no guilt. When you examine the selfishness and helplessness that is being justified by this approach, it can be seen that women who find themselves in this situation are being encouraged to remain passive and to take no responsibility for their lives, or to consider others. Take this quote from one of the other women: 'The Other Woman is not an ogre, she is just a woman who loves a man so much that she is willing to take what little she can get, live on the fringes of his life, and if that isn't true love, what is?' (*Daily Mail*, December 1982).

But love isn't about being a doormat. To behave in this unbalanced way is to have very little self-esteem. It raises questions of lack of identity and inability to create a happy life for oneself – even an un-conscious urge to seek unhappiness. True love involves two people who care for and respect the person they love whether they live with them or not. The caring and respect in this particular common situation are, sadly, all one way.

There is a strong element of self-labelling and labelling by society in the terms 'other woman' and 'mistress' which seems to encourage, or even create, a particular kind of stereotyped behaviour. A marriage counsellor, Chris Kell, said women allow themselves to be divided into either 'faithful wives at home' who 'ought' to be able to keep their men, or 'sexually disreputable women' but added: 'We are all capable of behaving in trustworthy and untrustworthy ways. We are all capable of having more than one relationship at the same time.

We choose situations. We are not different types of people' (*The Times*, 12 May 1995).

A journalist, writing about mistresses, said:

> *After talking to all these women I was left with the bizarre impression that they had all been talking about the same man. He was gentle and affectionate but hopelessly weak and indecisive . . . what's more, all these men apparently had the same wife. She was cold, distant, only wanted marriage for the social status and the children. She was middle-aged and had never lived alone, or worked . . . It turns each of them into crude caricatures, losing their individuality and their dignity, playing out this bad melodrama*

(Guardian, *31 October 1983*).

The promptings of the unconscious can lead us into all kinds of dilemmas. As we showed in the opening chapters, a person can have several sides to their nature with different energies that need expression. Those with a dual nature may be content with the person they married yet have affairs to satisfy an adventurous streak. However, this may have less to do with love than an inner drive that is attempting to integrate these two parts of their nature.

At a practical level there are attitudes and responsibilities to be looked at. If this is what, as an adult, you feel you need, has this need been made clear to your partner and have their feelings been taken into account? Are you prepared to allow them the same freedom if they need it? Marriage creates bonds at an emotional level which women generally take more seriously than men. To many men a 'one-night stand' is of little importance emotionally yet, if discovered, it can completely undermine a wife's trust. An affair can sometimes be dismissed in the same way. Men tend to underestimate the deep feelings and commitment that the majority of women bring to marriage. Even fleeting sexual relationships are rarely as casual for a woman as they seem, because her feelings are usually so much stronger than a man's. In a brief relationship or in marriage it is often the woman who is supplying most of the feelings. This is why it is so much easier for many men to walk out of a relationship, including marriage. Their desires may have been aroused but their feelings – the unconscious feminine side of their nature – will still be relatively dormant and therefore uncommitted.

Men have their feelings too, but find it difficult to talk about them with their men friends. In any case, for men to share their feelings with other men is generally discouraged in Western society. While women usually share aspects of their emotional life with their women friends, men are expected to channel their emotional life through their wife or female partner with all the ties that involves. One married man said of his lover: 'One of the most attractive things about this woman was her independence. She was financially successful, she wasn't going to depend on me' (*Guardian*, 11–12 September 1995).

An affair may be the first outward sign of an inward urge towards change in both men and women. Where the role, conventions and practical demands have taken over an excessive part of the whole, the psyche may rebel and, through external events, force a person to take note of the parts of their personality which are being neglected. Traditional marriage with its life-long commitment to one person is a very constraining institution when looked at in the light of the many variations in human nature. Until this century it appeared to work, though this may be more a function of social pressures and the fact that life expectancy was shorter. Society generally insisted on life-long marriage; roles were more clearly laid down and, of necessity, the majority of people were concerned with the means of survival, not the luxury of personal freedom or self-development.

For many people a lifetime of conventional monogamous marriage is ill-suited to the psyche's need for continuing change. When a person finds they have altered and their husband or wife is no longer a person they can relate to, or even blocks their individuality, life becomes complicated, creating deep dilemmas which go beyond society's moral attitudes. They may be very hard to resolve and cause great pain and difficulties however a person acts. There are no set solutions and it is for each person to act with responsibility and, as far as possible, in a caring way to minimise the pain. In Western culture divorce tends to be the main way that we can deal with affairs but this sometimes raises as many problems as it appears to solve.

It is when we take a look at attitudes to sex and marriage in other cultures that we can see how we create some of these stresses by our own deeply held beliefs about what marriage must be. Marriage and fidelity can be interpreted in different ways. The unrealistic demands that Blanche Lucas described look very different when set beside the views held by other societies. Duncan Pryde (1972), in a book about his life with the Inuit (Eskimos) of Arctic Canada, wrote: 'Eskimos don't think of sex in the romantic way we do. An Eskimo woman doesn't fall head over heels in love as we would say. Marriage is a practical matter to her, and sex is something else again.'

Pryde described their openness about extra-marital sex in some detail, showing how anger, jealousy and guilt, so common in the West, are of much less importance in a society with a different moral code. 'There was no question of adultery or any feeling of shame . . . As long as a man or woman chooses someone outside his or her kinship circle, any arrangement agreeable to the persons concerned was possible.'

He found that though some Inuit men and women were promis-cuous, most of these relationships were exchanges between husbands and wives, the product of comradeship in a hostile land. Various conventions had to be observed but the main rule was to ask first. 'Normally, a man would never ask for an exchange relationship unless he were virtually certain the woman's husband would agree. Nor would he risk an illicit arrangement unless he was prepared for a violent reaction.'

Pryde, a single man, found himself invited into a relationship by Niksaaktuq, the eager young wife of Nasarlulik, a hunting companion and close friend, with Nasarlulik's full agreement. 'Do you desire my wife? Well, Niksaaktuq likes you and I like you too, so if you want to get my wife (and that was the term he used) then go ahead.'

Where two men shared a wife in this way, Pryde wrote, the men's relationship deepened and each also took on responsibility for the welfare of the other and his dependants should he fall ill. Although this approach to sexual relations developed as part of one society's means of surviving in a harsh climate, it shows that our own, more comfortable, society may have something to learn about dealing with a married couple's individual emotional needs and the sexual feelings which exist independently of marriage.

One way in which some couples in our society express these sexual needs is by joining organised sex parties where each chooses a partner for the evening. Unlike the Inuit people described, not all these couples have a relationship strong enough to withstand the emotional risks. Agony columns in some of the popular press occasionally feature a letter from a partner (usually a wife) asking how she can resist her husband's request to go to one of these parties, or avoid going again having tried the experience.

Here again, it seems to depend on the relationship. A woman married for twenty years said: 'The reason we went into "swinging" is that there are only so many things you can do with sex and two people . . . It's not that we fell out of love with each other, you just want that cherry on the cake.' She added though: 'This is no recipe for a dodgy marriage. You need to be strong together from the start. If there is any weakness there, doing this will destroy it (*Today*, 25 October 1995).

Affairs so often create havoc and unhappiness and act as a prelude to divorce that the more positive changes an affair can produce are rarely noticed. Moral and social values create a climate in which the betrayal and transgression involved overshadow the affair's function in a wider sense. We fail to acknowledge, as the Inuit have done, that a person, though married, may still need to develop through intimate – and not always sexual – relationships with others.

People need to achieve intimacy throughout life, and with both sexes, but it very often happens that an intimate relationship with someone of the opposite sex naturally progresses into a sexual one. A sexual relationship often initiates a learning process whether we want this or not. And so one sexual relationship in adult life may be insufficient to meet our needs at this level of learning – where our unconscious is prompting us. The psyche's urge to become whole so that we use our capacities more completely is not easily denied and falling in love in 'forbidden' circumstances becomes a test of our deeper convictions.

The responsibility that Duncan Pryde talks about is an important factor in any affair. To balance personal needs against commitments and responsibilities creates deep dilemmas because the need for relationship is so strong. It is the premium that we place on the sexual act which obscures this issue so that divorce tends to be the automatic 'solution'. Or is it?

When to tell your partner that you are having an affair is another dilemma. An affair so often follows a build-up of difficulties in a marriage, of which either one or both partners may be aware. The person having the affair very often knows that there are problems in the marriage and even knows what they are. If they tell their partner, in a sense it is another way of bringing up their differences, a subject that needed to be raised earlier. This at last gives an opportunity to deal with the problems though it may be too late and too difficult by then to regain an emotional understanding. In this context the affair may be the tip of a very large iceberg, or a much smaller one when the couple can talk through the crisis and reach a new understanding. Cries of infidelity, of being deceived, which accompany many such revelations, may be hollow when set beside a long chapter of discord, upset or indifference which preceded the act itself.

Some couples are able to find a means of coping and working with the issues when one is having an affair.

> Jack became aware after some time that Tina was having a relationship with someone else. He was as much puzzled as hurt by what was happening but would not raise the subject directly. There was no row, no recriminations. Instead Jack elected to stand back and let Tina sort out what she wanted without any pressure from him. The affair finally ended, and although Jack did not want to face the reasons behind it stemming from the marriage, they reached a different understanding and stayed together.

In some cases open revelations may be the best thing that could happen despite the difficulties they raise. A marriage in which the person having the affair preserves the normal routine while suppressing feelings of discontent creates powerful undercurrents that may be sensed by the other partner and by children. The feeling of having to maintain a surface respectability but living a lie produces pressures which often manifest in acute guilt. Fear of the partner's response and the trouble that will ensue adds to this guilt which may become unendurable. A person may then lose the initiative of revealing the affair at a moment of their choosing so that instead the knowledge bursts out uncontrollably – though they may in effect allow themselves to be found out. Paul's experience shows one way in which this happens:

> 'I had a number of affairs over several years and even though this must have been obvious, Sue never seemed to notice. Our

life of routine just continued. Then I started with someone who lived in the house exactly opposite. Inevitably Sue saw me leaving late one night and all my feelings came up into the open. I realised later I must have used this affair to force something to happen in the marriage. Now we are getting divorced.'

We don't always have the courage to act responsibly when it is necessary. Consideration for the others involved in such complex areas of our lives is difficult to achieve, and the priorities are hard to define because we do not want to hurt other people or risk what we have. How we give and receive at intimate levels is an area of emotional relationship that we are only beginning to explore and understand.

CHAPTER FIVE

Talking and Making Decisions

Conflicting emotions surface when a marriage appears to be near its end and this is a new and often frightening experience. A few people can distance themselves sufficiently and others can appear to. The feelings of confusion, guilt, anger, jealousy and perhaps fear which now erupt make it difficult to act calmly. Deep feelings of desperate loneliness can overtake and engulf everything. You may feel simply unable to cope with everyday living – you may burst out crying, feel physically ill, or your body may just ache all over. At work you may sit in a daze unable to concentrate, leisure activities may be undertaken listlessly or with aggressive concentration, and at home with the family the atmosphere can be strained and distant, or argumentative.

Once this situation is reached it is time to break the patterns of disagreement and seek a new understanding of the problem. Human nature being what it is, we hope the problem will go away or get better of its own accord. But there is no use in just wishing things were better. At this stage of an unhappy relationship leaving things any longer only makes them worse. The best route is to face the crisis and start working through the real issues, which may be obvious or still hidden behind a facade. This may make it necessary for one person to take the initiative to resolve things.

We recognise that to try to break this deadlock can seem impossible. This very sensitive and complex area of human relations is one about which there are no easy answers. But you must ask yourself honestly whether you are simply going through a bad patch, or whether the time has come to face reality and accept that the marriage could be over. We know from personal experience the tremendous emotional and practical pressures that arise once a person wants to do something about the problems of a deeply unhappy marriage. The emotional reactions cannot be predicted and changes that come now are profound and possibly irrevocable. These can mark the start of a long period of intense personal struggle in which there may be all kinds of setbacks. You may wonder at times whether it is all worth while; yet it is possible to build up a sense of certainty and confidence that your life can be changed for the better.

There are important reasons for taking progressive steps now to reach a conclusion. It is unnerving and unsettling to live in a strained atmosphere for long because it invades all your thoughts and actions; it affects your self-esteem and sense of security; and the well-being of children may be affected. This approach to a relationship, which might be new to you, is an essential theme of this chapter. It involves actively caring for yourself and dealing with your partner in the same directed, practical way you might try to overcome a serious difficulty with a friend, at work or elsewhere in the family. It is important to remember that this approach to marriage problems is valid at all times of life. The difficulties of divorcing at sixty may well be much more than those at thirty or forty, but the need for fulfilment and happiness is similar and can be sought and found at any age.

It is tempting here to pretend that everything is not all that bad. People are often prepared to put up with ways of living and all kinds of behaviour that they would not expect a friend facing similar problems to accept so that even impossible circumstances, which may include mental or physical abuse, will continue for as long as people will continue to put up with them. Yet, while this is going on, anger and resentment build up underneath and the entire situation can worsen in at least two ways: any remaining chance that you could stay together will be lost; and so much anger may build up that the divorce can only be a bitter one. Here, physical separation from your partner, such as a weekend away, can provide a breathing space to allow these feelings to be faced.

In this chapter we aim to show how getting to grips with the issues is both necessary and beneficial – and how it is possible to escape the pattern of unhappy marriage. There are some very useful techniques for bringing the issues out into the open and talking constructively to resolve them once and for all so that you can get on with living your life. For those in the most extreme situations, such as physical and emotional violence, we suggest ways of achieving some resolution based on the same principles.

It is very hard to try to understand the conflicting emotions which well up, such as the exasperation, anger and resentment that so many of us cannot help feeling. Understandably, we are not very good at talking about a sensitive emotional issue to someone else because we have never been trained to do it. Our feelings tend to take us over so that even minor issues become exaggerated in our minds and the big ones frighten us. Somehow, as we showed when we discussed ways of arguing (in the chapter on unhappy marriage), we must find constructive ways to say what we have to say and not be satisfied until answers are reached. This has to be a gradual, step-by-step process; it cannot happen overnight. It may take many weeks or months to arrive at a solution. But the most important factor is the approach and attitude you adopt. There may be different ways of meeting the difficulties yet there is a particular approach which works. It involves adopting positive attitudes, which can be described as: constructive, flexible, non-accusative and geared to problem solving. As we showed earlier in the book, there are two kinds of arguments, constructive and destructive ones. Similarly there are constructive and destructive ways of solving the present problems.

It is easier to talk about this than to carry it out since we instinctively blame and hit back, usually refusing to take *our* share of the responsibility. We readily see where the other person is at fault – in other words we externalise the problems which, really, come from within the *two* people involved. Therefore, whatever the other person's actions, nothing can ever be wholly the other person's fault. It is very painful to ask yourself what part you have played, but to get anywhere satisfactorily it is necessary to do so.

A very common, and often hidden, pattern to consider is whether there is too much interdependence between you and your partner. As we have said, any close relationship involves taking roles and these may become too set and potentially unhealthy. It is an issue the American psychiatrist M. Scott Peck regards as stemming from a confusion in people's minds about the nature of love. He believes it is healthy when couples deliberately change their usual roles and division of labour to create variety in their marriage. But, he points out, this is not merely play but 'is a process that diminishes their mutual dependency even if done unconsciously' (Peck, 1988).

Here is an opportunity to consider whether this could be an issue. Does one of you occasionally do a task, such as cooking a meal or washing the car, that the other person 'always' does? Does one of you usually resist doing such a task – perhaps because you see it as a 'man's job' or a 'woman's job'? If so, a look at your belief system may help you break a deadlock.

Affairs are one of the most painful issues in marriage and may force a couple to look closely at their relationship and to face the possibility of divorce. However, as we showed in our chapter on affairs, they are not as simple as they seem and divorce is not necessarily a solution. Before divorce is even considered the upset and highly charged atmosphere needs to be allowed to settle. This gives time to establish how serious a threat the affair is to the marriage. Initially it may be regarded, by all involved, as simply giving in to temptation. Many affairs are conducted only at this level – the word itself throws up an instant image. You may have to decide where you stand on this particular issue and act accordingly. But there is more going on at another level whether it is realised or not; to try to understand the importance of a particular affair or affairs at the emotional level makes it easier to reach decisions.

Is the affair perhaps a 'necessary' one which is giving a man or woman experiences they feel they have missed in their earlier years before marriage? It may be a passing phase no matter how intense the affair is, even for a partner who moves out to live with someone else. Many a dramatic relationship of this kind fizzles out in the reality of everyday living. Or is it part of a pattern, a restless streak in your partner's nature? If so, you are faced with a choice of accepting this behaviour and that marriage may not be a big commitment to them, or of refusing to accept it. Is it a much stronger relationship which your partner needs in addition to the marriage or instead of it? Or you may be in this situation yourself. It may be that one of you has reached a point in your emotional development where a different kind of relationship is important. One vital area is the question of each person's needs and whether they are being met. If, say, you feel you are being given no affection or find it difficult to give your partner affection, this must be raised. It is the crucial area of needs which must be frankly discussed and not merely the event itself.

There is no one solution to these dilemmas, but there is always a point at which you have to make a decision and act on it. People react in many different ways so before you act in haste consider other people's experiences. For some their partner's first affair ends the marriage as far as they are concerned. Others will accept and some merely tolerate a series of affairs and achieve a different balance in their relationship. Much depends on a person's needs and their level of maturity. One wife accepted two separate affairs her husband had and continued the relationship. But when he announced for the third time that he was seeing someone else she decided categorically that enough was enough and started divorce proceedings. She asked him to move out and though this affair also ended she stuck to her decision and refused to have him back.

When passions are high or the situation intolerable, it is extremely difficult to take that one step back and try to clarify your needs. From here you may begin to work towards what you want. This takes time. To make a hasty decision, like walking out of the house or deciding, in anger, to divorce is only a short-term solution and one almost certain to inflame matters. To leave a relationship, then properly disengage from it, is a far more complex process. To work through this process makes it easier eventually to reach an agreement which allows both partners to resolve their differences with dignity and on reasonable terms. This is crucial where children are involved because the repercussions may last *their* lifetime as well as yours if they have to share the burden of your continuing animosity.

Talking to the other person can raise its own problems according to their temperament. Some people will deny that anything is wrong, others can only shout when any subject involving the feelings is raised. There are people who are always convinced they are right and some who act in a bullying and authoritarian way whenever anything is discussed; those to whom any criticism strikes at their pride and still others who, when things go wrong, are never there to face the consequences.

One of the commonest problems here is to know what to say to your partner and especially how to begin. Although strong feelings may colour your attitude, try to put together the different aspects so that you can raise the issues at stake and put them in a measured way. To get a response you could state frankly: 'I'm upset and worried about our relationship and that you won't discuss it with me. I may be assuming things which are not the case such as . . . and I want to know. Could we please find time to talk about it?' This approach makes it less likely that you will merely complain about each other and go round in circles, never getting beyond the accusations. You could also say: 'It's hard to say this, but I've realised for some time that things have changed between us. I am not happy and there is something I want to say . . .' This involves telling your partner what is on your mind and asking them what they are feeling or thinking.

It helps to time your approach. A legacy of difficulties going back over several months or years cannot be resolved in one evening and there are right and wrong times to discuss them. Few people are in the right mood to talk immediately after a day's work in or outside the home. It is far better to wait until you have eaten a meal and rested before raising the subject. Then sit down, in chairs at the same level, and begin to talk. This immediately involves both of you in the discussion and allows direct eye contact. To try to discuss important issues while doing some other task, or at bedtime when tired, defeats the object of achieving direct communication. But privacy is all-important. If there are children or relatives in the house, wait until they are in bed or, better still, choose a time when everyone is out. If necessary, make an 'appointment' to talk at a specific time.

One of the most difficult responses to deal with is where a partner maintains a silence and will not discuss anything. There may be fear behind their unwillingness to confront the problems, or plain obstinacy. Because differences in temperament become exaggerated, a reliable friend could 'interpret' how you are feeling and some progress may be made this way. If you feel able, some reassurance through a gentle approach may enable you to open a discussion about the change in the relationship. If this approach does not work, it leaves you with little alternative but to explain, perhaps in a written note, that you intend to take some initiative to improve matters. Making this move may produce a response but where it does not you have to act for your own well-being. One woman whose kind but uncomprehending husband refused to enter any conversation about the rift in their marriage said: 'I wish now I had shouted at him to

make him take notice because he would not see how unhappy I was.'
He was unable to see that her needs had changed and they later
divorced.

The situation where a partner will not discuss anything, or denies
that anything is wrong with the relationship, is one which many
wives in particular have to face. The phlegmatic, dutiful husband who
works hard to provide for the family may well see his role mainly as
a provider and be more concerned with the protocols of family life
than with the emotional undercurrents, which to him may be
irrelevant. He may not even be aware of them. For these reasons his
wife may be left to act out the emotional and feeling elements of his
life for him and so he underestimates her capacity to function as an
independent person with needs of her own. This undercurrent can
show itself in several ways as, for example, in his resentment if she
returns to work after many years running a home.

In a marriage with set roles of this kind, a woman who is changing
and wants to express herself more fully after years of being 'the
dependent wife' may find it very difficult to convey to her husband
what is happening to her. She has to struggle against the impasse and
against the inertia of her own role in the marriage. Since she may
have left the decision-making parts of the marriage to her husband,
her attempts to assert herelf and make changes are very much a
personal struggle. As her awareness of the rift grows she is likely to
feel an inner inevitability, mixed with guilt and loneliness, that she
has to stand on her own. This brings with it the realisation that, if a
break-up occurs, it will involve the loss of status and the security she
has enjoyed and which have been a major part of her identity up to
now. She will have to find a new sense of identity within herself.

For both women and men who find it difficult to stand up for
themselves and say what they mean, learning to be assertive (but not
aggressive) is one answer. By joining an assertiveness class you can
safely act out confrontational situations in role play, and experience
how it feels to be successful – supported by feedback from the trainer
and class.

The partner who can only shout when any issue to do with the
feelings is raised is also denying that anything must alter in the
marriage. A man whose feelings are just beneath the surface may
react very quickly indeed to anything he feels is disruptive. To him

the idea of a serious talk about marriage is likely to be seen as very threatening. Even where there is no clash, no arguments or little said, one or both partners may not want to delve into the real issues, or be unable to. Unless there is some kind of breakthrough, such as beginning to exchange feelings or accepting help, it becomes extremely difficult to repair the rift by finding common ground. Without this, any real relationship now simply dies although many couples who reach this point stay together and maintain the marriage.

Difficulties in marriage so strongly affect our sense of self-esteem and sense of status at such a fundamental level that they uncover the less pleasant sides of our character. European and Japanese societies in particular put so much emphasis on being 'nice' and 'polite' to others that the aggressive energy which is in all of us and often repressed may be powerfully released when a marriage goes wrong. A normally kindly person may become physically dangerous. Sadness, frustrations and depression may now surface so that the personality undergoes a complete change.

It is so easy to get caught up in disagreements that anger hides the opportunities to deal with them in a mature, adult way. It is easy to continue blaming the other person and directing your resentment at them. They may be doing the same to you and each of you may not even consider your part in the problem. But the potential for angry and difficult behaviour exists in all of us and can take us over. However, it is only a part of our personality and the other, more positive, sides are still there. When you are not getting on with somebody don't let the 'bad' side of their nature cut you off from this 'good' side. They are both part of the same person. To remember this creates the opportunity to relate to them on a level which leads to resolution.

How well you truly know your partner can make a crucial difference to how you get through to them. Everybody has a positive side to their nature which can respond when the right approach is made. One person will respond to an appeal to their sense of fairness, another to their compassion. A person with a competitive spirit might respond to a challenge to achieve a solution. This is all part of the skills of understanding and communication which you will have to develop at this time. To make yourself clear, express only what you are fed up with and what you want for yourself. The words you use are important since people tend to be taken over by their emotional reactions to what they hear. For this reason, words have to be chosen with care. Arguments are one thing but exchanging insults, or opinionated views, achieves the opposite effect since this results in using words which only inflame.

All this involves trying to assess yourself and your own feelings and needs beyond the anger and frustration that are almost inevitably present. The skill with which you do this will decide to a great extent the way events progress towards a well-intentioned solution. It makes little difference whether you are angry or upset by what your partner may have done, or the other way round; it is still necessary to get beyond the anger in order to communicate. Where there is a lot of emotion present it is extremely hard to establish and accept the truth of the situation. Perhaps someone else does not want to admit they are having an affair, or a partner may feel their behaviour is being questioned in some other way.

Arguments may be necessary to relieve true feelings and clear the air. However, people's ability to express their feelings varies widely. While some people will control them, others bottle them up so that they erupt under stress, making communication difficult, if not impossible. The build-up of unexpressed feelings and its release are behind many acts such as irrational outbursts, physical violence against a partner and child battering. With effort and some goodwill on both sides progress can be achieved in all but extreme circumstances. By applying the suggestions we have made and looking at methods of your own, better ways of communication can be found.

One unhappy wife, who finally left, realised that for years there had been a pattern in which her husband coped easily with criticism but responded best to praise. She used this knowledge to improve the atmosphere between them by reducing her criticism of him and giving praise where it was due.

When a partner refuses to acknowledge that there is a problem, and will not discuss it, then if this attitude persists you may have to consider forcing the issue in some way if anything is to change. You could have made some assumptions that are not entirely right, but nevertheless you cannot know how you stand without some feedback.

By now you may feel the need to speak to a lawyer to consider the legal options open to you. You will have to make a judgement whether to tell your partner you are taking this step or wait until you feel the moment is right. It could be that it is only when you tell your partner you have seen a lawyer that they realise you are no longer prepared to let matters drift.

To realise without warning that your partner considers the marriage is over and is planning to leave can come only as a severe shock, and a devastating one if your partner has suddenly left. The abrupt transformation of normal life into upset and uncertainty immediately makes an emotional mark which can last a long time.

The initial feelings of shock, bewilderment and disbelief can be considerable. There may be other feelings too: anger and a fierce sense of betrayal, particularly if your partner is involved with someone else. After the first blow it is very hard to even believe the reality of what is happening, or make any sense of it.

If you are the person who has been left, whether or not you were aware that this was going to happen, your position is one of passivity. Your partner has made the active decision to go and and you have not been given a choice. Though the early feelings of shock and bewilderment are more acute when a partner leaves without obvious warning, we believe that if this happens some changes in the relationship will have occurred. You might not have been aware of them or have picked up the signals. It could be that you realised that something was wrong in your relationship but did not talk about it or deal with it in any direct way. You may have dismissed this notion, feeling that the marriage was safe and 'it could never happen to me'. Feelings of anger and vulnerability you may now have are mixed with those of both blaming your partner and a sense of some responsibility for causing the breakdown.

Marriages and live-in relationships are built on trust and this is strained to the limit when your partner wants to leave. It is important to try to preserve and even rebuild the trust element, which may break down altogether unless you can see the real person through your emotional upset. Remember, your relationship has been trusting in the past and many areas of trust can remain if you allow it. The development of some form of trust from this point is crucial, because it will help to determine the possibility of reconciliation or the sensible handling of divorce. This is a period of great confusion, but remember that no one person is at fault, nor is one of you wholly to blame for what has happened – and time does heal. These words will not take away the pain and upset you may be feeling and you might need a friend, counsellor, your minister or a doctor to help you to cope.

It takes courage to begin to accept what has happened to you and to recognise some of the patterns of the relationship which have led to the parting. You might have to accept that your partner does not want to come back and the truth will hurt. They may be leaving you for someone else after having considered it for some time. Yet there is a positive side when a relationship breaks down in this way, because gradually you *can* come to know yourself more completely and feel secure.

You may desperately want the marriage to continue, and any talking you are able to do will bring your views into the open and could give you a different perspective. Your partner may tell you that they feel something has been missing. Whether or not you can accept this, it is important to try to express your own feelings. Depending on the kind of person he or she is, you may be given explicit reasons why they want to leave; or they may be unable, or not want, to communicate. They may not do so to spare your feelings or avoid an argument.

Your partner might simply feel an urgent need for a breathing space, after years of being together, in which to find themselves and to consider their future. They may not have been able to tell you this as they might not have recognized it themselves. The urge to break out in this way sometimes comes quite unexpectedly.

> Brenda, who was in her forties and comfortably married, found herself saying, out of the blue, to a friend one day: 'I am going to leave my husband'. This was the first time she was aware of these feelings. Her women friends understood but her men friends found her intentions 'unthinkable'. A personal struggle now began as Brenda came to realise that she had unused talents to explore and needed complete independence. She and her husband did divorce.

If you are considering leaving your partner, then try to imagine first how you might feel or react if this happened to you. It is one of the most powerful ways you can reject someone and it can severely shake their self-confidence. You might feel unable to tell your partner the truth and face the possible reactions but it could save a good deal of bitterness to give some warning of what you are planning – unless threats to your safety leave you with no alternative. There could be aspects of your relationship that you have not even considered and which you would benefit from knowing. To talk will probably release tensions which have been present for a long time. By not doing this now it is difficult to avoid carrying an unconscous burden of unspoken thoughts which upset your emotional life and can lead to regret.

To leave suddenly denies your partner the opportunity to begin to work through feelings of rejection. These may exist on both sides – the person who leaves may have felt rejected during the relationship, while the person who is left faces rejection when it breaks up.

Whatever the circumstances, the person you are leaving will be very hurt and find it difficult to believe what you say. It is now up to you to show ways in which you can still be trusted and be reliable over any arrangements that have to be made. For example, if you are supposed to pay financial support, provide it as promised. If there is an arrangement for contact with children, stick to it as far as possible so that the children are ready to be collected/returned, or that you collect and return them at the agreed time. Trust established at this practical level helps to reduce friction at an emotional level.

Occasionally there seems to be no alternative to leaving abruptly. For some people this may be the only way to break the bond of their relationship, which to them has become meaningless or destructive. By making this choice you are taking a course which has its own obvious difficulties; yet the practical and emotional adjustments needed still cannot be denied. After having achieved the physical and emotional distance you can set your mind to dealing with all the ensuing problems of separation.

If you are left behind and continue to love your partner, and cannot bear them going, you may hope as time passes that they will come back. Occasionally this happens, with one or more attempts at reconciliation, but you will have to judge when to accept that there will be no permanent reconciliation. A gut feeling may tell you that the marriage is over but it is often better not to make any hard decision about this for some time since the situation remains an open one while emotions are worked through. Since you are forced into doing things independently, you can gain valuable confidence by putting this to use. Often separation gradually shades towards a more permanent state as daily habits begin to change. Meanwhile, use the chance now presented to take a hard look at yourelf, perhaps with outside help.

It can take months, even several years, for someone to come to terms with the reasons why their partner wanted to leave. It is possible to accept that your partner wants something different in life. If you are the one who has decided to go, it may take patient talking to explain your feelings, but a point is reached eventually where explanations have to stop and the other person has to cope with their feelings. Do try to keep a bridge of communication open. This can be done through a friend or through the contact which is made in looking after children.

What we are suggesting may appear to be a completely new approach to dealing with problems. It may be that the openness of earlier years has been lost, so it requires time and persistence to re-establish this kind of exchange – or to learn it for the first time. The aim is to clarify the situation and this could involve going over a lot of ground about what led up to recent events. The initial reaction may be very emotional or deadpan, or your questions may be pushed aside and this can block your first attempts to open a discussion. But don't be put off talking since nothing can be resolved without being frank.

Although we talked at some length about arguments and ways of communicating in the chapter on unhappy marriage, we feel strongly the need to enlarge upon this theme here. If we were asked to summarise this approach in a few words they would be: step back; establish what you want and *communicate*. These ground rules are worth supplementing with a few do's and don'ts:

Don't make constant accusations	Do express your feelings
Don't swap insults and put downs	Do create a dialogue
	Do be honest
Don't hide the real issues	Do stand up for yourself
Don't be a doormat	Do try to be flexible
Don't reject any positive ideas	Do remember that you
Don't forget that time *does* heal	were both happy once

Throughout this book we are offering a number of ideas and approaches to handling what are complex circumstances but, nevertheless, the scales are often loaded in different ways against both men and women. Many men find it extremely difficult, and some practically impossible, to express their feelings to their partners. Instead, their feelings may be held back by a mask of traditional behaviour which is difficult to penetrate. This, in part, is what drives many wives to the point where they seek care and affection elsewhere. Equally, for many women, it is still extremely difficult, and for some practically impossible, to assert themselves to say what they want, and to achieve individuality beyond the role their husband requires of them. This, paradoxically, drives many husbands eventually into relationships with women who give and take on a more equal basis. However, it may not always work out like this. Sometimes what seems to be a totally new kind of relationship can turn out to have a similar pattern to the last.

Deep ingrained attitudes reinforced by society's stereotypes of marriage roles are often huge stumbling blocks to couples in a crisis and may even provoke it. Lack of awareness of themselves beyond these roles and of the part that feelings and assertion plays in everyday life creates misunderstandings for both sexes and prevents a true dialogue.

People find many reasons for not taking the steps to free themselves from a relationship they believe is empty. Their inner knowledge that it has effectively ended is opposed by all kinds of thoughts and principles which make them hang on and be reluctant to leave. For example, a strict belief that a marriage should never be dissolved may itself be a rigid attitude which traps them. Some people strongly resist any idea of leaving because any loss of status and standard of living is unthinkable to them. It *is* a huge decision to leave because it is likely to be the most complicated and distressing change we are to make in our lives. The ramifications can extend into almost every area of a couple's lives, forcing changes in personal relationships, family networks, work patterns, and bring domestic as well as emotional upheavals. Further, the values to which you may have held firmly may be turned upside down, so that you are forced to see life differently. It is at this point that you may decide to divorce.

There are many common fears and apprehensions which surface at this time and they can have such a paralysing effect that a person may stay in an empty marriage for years before they finally go, or never leave it. These feelings are powerful because often they relate to habits, views and attitudes which belong to us as individuals, to our sense of who we are. To resolve a marriage crisis you may have to say 'no' or make a painful choice for the first time in your life. This may also involve adopting attitudes very different to some you held before.

The feelings which arise and are common to many are fears of the unknown, of being alone, not knowing where you will live or what the future will hold, and the belief that you will be no happier anywhere else. You may be afraid to face the disapproval of family and friends and worry about the children's future. You may also want to cling to the home and lifestyle you have become accustomed to over the years. These insecurities bind us to the situation we are in and test our ability to work through the problems and get our priorities right. If the prospect of staying together is intolerable it is helpful to understand that the doubts and insecurities we have may be blinding us to how things could be different in other circumstances. The fear of being alone does not mean that you will be alone – new friends soon appear in the life of someone who does their best to make a new start, even if some old ones are lost. The belief that you can be no happier anywhere else is not only being pessimistic but allowing your doubts to block your self-confidence. These doubts deny your capacity to create a happier life elsewhere. Leaving what you know and what is familiar is harder the older you become, but you may still have to do it.

The disappointment that family and friends are bound to feel when they learn of a couple's decision to break up can strongly inhibit some people from making any change. A person who is aware that most of their friends see them and their partner as 'happily married' – perhaps the ideal couple – find it very hard to admit openly that the relationship is otherwise. Worries that a break-up will be met by disappointment and disapproval are very real, because the situation itself may touch off insecurities in others, even including colleagues at work. These feelings in others have to be acknowledged but nevertheless what is necessary for the individual, and the couple, needs to be worked through. Although divorce has now touched very many families, relatives and friends nevertheless cannot be fully aware of the deeper emotional interactions in the relationship.

Apart from the natural upset, in some families the disapproval of relatives presents enormous pressures and obstacles to someone trying hard to resolve their problems. The first mention of separation or divorce may be treated as a betrayal of shared values. However, the sense of guilt that can be induced to keep 'the family' intact at all costs is essentially a form of manipulation which denies a couple in difficulties the right to control their own destiny. This is a very different attitude from the genuine family concern in which parents and other relatives may offer help and understanding without interfering.

It can be deeply upsetting to contemplate the effect of a break-up on those close to us such as elderly parents, and how the lives of children might be changed with only one parent at home. We tend to forget, though, that children can be resilient despite the hardships and, with help and reassurance, better able to cope than we imagine. We talk further about children's responses and how they cope in Chapter 7.

Marriage break-up can make us feel vulnerable and insecure in many ways of which one of the most alarming can be our worries about material status. Many of us become so attached and used to our home and lifestyle that we imagine our world falling apart for ever if these are threatened by the radical change that divorce brings – to the extent that this may be the major reason we cannot leave when all other indications say we should. Yet someone to whom a settled or particular lifestyle is important may be the person best motivated to establish these things quickly elsewhere – once they have made the break. One of their needs may be to become aware of this.

Concerns like these which make us hang on are often related to elements of our personality which we need to confront and work through to gain a better perspective and balance within ourselves. The break-up process itself exposes these very difficulties in our makeup and also produces the opportunities to do something about them. So there is a two-fold process here; one involves achieving as an individual the inner strength and security needed to start resolving particular emotional blocks and the other is using this approach to deal with the relationship problems of separation and divorce. They are so closely intertwined that they become as one. This is a challenge which not everyone realises exists and can accept, but it is primarily an opportunity which enables both partners to change and develop, though one may change more than the other.

It can be frightening to realise that it is necessary to come to grips with emotional situations which are completely new, but amidst the confusion this is a period of subtle change which, if recognised, can lead to new attitudes and greater self-confidence which will make the important changes easier. During this period a conflict with other feelings may make us resist change. For example, parents understandably find the effect of a break-up on their children difficult to cope with, even when they first consider it. It is felt keenly by both fathers and mothers although men often don't show it. The wives, and husbands, who stay in a marriage 'for the sake of the children' are rightly concerned about their welfare because they love them. But when this becomes an over-riding concern it may deny other necessary areas of life which would enable a mother or father to achieve a balance and so lead a more satisfying life. The price, though, may have to be the break-up of the family and it may be a devastating choice to face. The many men who leave their families without apparent thought (and women too) may be denying the inevitable feelings of concern that are present, even if they are unaware of them. That these feelings exist is revealed partly in the problems which arise when a man who has walked out suddenly snatches the children, or takes an intense interest in them after a gap of months or even years without any contact.

A woman who always puts her family's needs first and ignores her own, or a man who always puts his own needs first and ignores those of his family have each to achieve a balance so that they value both themselves and others.

Similarly money, which may have produced problems for a long time, can be a real and crucial obstacle to leaving. The loss of financial support and the hardship which may occur if a partner leaves are sufficient to block expression of the underlying feelings which could help them deal with the prospect of break-up. However, our everyday lives and comforts can sometimes be an illusion in which our deeper disappointments and aspirations are put aside or repressed.

If you would far rather leave things as they are than have to cope with markedly reduced circumstances following break-up, consider why you are making this choice. It may be hard to judge which is the higher price to pay, whether to leave and be worse off financially or stay and suffer deep frustrations which eventually may become impossible to control. But many people who leave, or are left, find that they are a lot happier in spite of the hardships. In any case income and status fluctuate and financial security is far from guaranteed for anyone in today's difficult economic conditions. Incomes can rise as well as fall in changed circumstances. Despite the practicalities of little money there may be a lesson to learn that involves attitudes about money's real importance. These attitudes can be revealed in many simple and apparently quite rational statements. For example, the man who, though his marriage is finished, tells his girlfriend that he will not leave his wife because he cannot afford to is effectively saying he values his bank balance more than anything else. This is ironic considering that should his wife leave *him* he would have to face the financial difficulties anyway.

The conflicting feelings a person has to deal with at the point they decide to break up can be shared with a friend, a relative or even someone they meet casually who has a sympathetic ear. Some people are naturally good counsellors. They are able to listen and often provide a way to see the problems more clearly. Though the listener may do nothing by way of giving advice they provide a sounding board which enables others to get in touch with their emotions. This is unlikely to provide any instant solutions but the act of expressing your feelings out loud helps to release them. Confiding in someone leads towards greater understanding and helps to give a focus so that you can act.

You may be fortunate enough to know somebody who has the rare quality of being a good listener without making judgements when faced with someone else's problems. But be wary. People generally have built-in biases to their attitudes and are more likely to give unhelpful though well-meaning advice, or take sides, especially if they are close friends or relatives. Well-worn statements such as: 'All men are the same', 'You can never understand a woman', or 'If I were you . . .' have no value and only perpetuate disagreements.

A trial separation is one way to find the emotional and physical space many people need to come to terms with the difficulties of the past months or years. It is a big step to take but may be the one way to break free from repetitive patterns of disagreement and begin to see the realities before you consider whether or not the relationship is worth preserving. It may be, though, that while one person begins to experience a considerable change of attitude the other continues to dwell on the old patterns of disagreement. This is a fluctuating period of relief mixed with doubts and anxieties and brings up many added worries at the same time: the practical ones of money; where to live; concern about children as well as the continuing turmoil over the relationship. For both the partner who moves out and the one who stays at home there may be many new anxieties to add to those about the relationship.

This may be one of the toughest periods of your life, whether the separation is temporary or permanent. Feelings of guilt, depression and vulnerability arise which involve your whole being and can lead some people into reactions such as withdrawal or frantic socialising. For some it is a traumatic period of pure survival. These feelings are expressed by many people who go through divorce. They affect some more profoundly than others so that each person has to find their own way through. Within your daily activities and social life you may have a deep sense of being alone. Though these feelings may be intermittent this makes them no less hard to bear, yet they can have a purpose. Learning to stand alone touches our greatest vulnerabilities but can also reach an inner strength which is in each of us. This involves our ability to understand what is exposed in us, and to achieve greater security in these untouched aspects of our individuality. Monica Furlong has written:

> We need to pick ourselves up and begin life again, with guts and determination, trying new things, meeting new people, recognising that within that marriage whole parts of our personality lay fallow (they do within any marriage) and that now we have a new opportunity to discover more about ourselves

> (Furlong, 1981)

By being adventurous we become stronger within ourselves and the experience can lay the foundations for new relationships.

All the difficulties we have been talking about in this chapter may appear at times so insurmountable that you seem to be getting nowhere. There may be moments of great happiness and freedom – perhaps for the first time in years – but also days of deep despair, loneliness, regret and even panic. But gradually as time passes you begin to feel alive again. Your 'progress' depends on how much you are able to resolve both the practical difficulties and the emotional conflicts within yourself. A great many people go through a long heart-searching phase extending from before separation to beyond divorce which may last for a period of several years. Sharing the difficulties of separation and divorce with others can help to provide a route through them but taking advantage of professional help aids the process. Problems can be explored in sessions with a counsellor. Sometimes distress can manifest in different ways at any stage of a relationship difficulty. Many doctors, psychologists and other health professionals find that patients come to them with various physical symptoms which are expressions of their inner emotional turmoil.

Some of the biggest problems of divorce arise directly from the haphazard and uncaring way in which many break-ups occur. You can still do what needs to be done yet in a better way which minimises as far as you can the inevitable upset and upheaval. For example, it is unkind to leave a partner just before Christmas unless there is no other course to take. Similarly, to go shortly before a family holiday which children have been looking forward to only creates additional upset. This is different from simply putting off the actual moment of leaving. If you have resolved to go and have made this clear then, in one sense, the pressure is relieved and you can try to time the event to suit the circumstances.

> Jessica considered her husband's position as a public figure and realised it would be kinder to wait and leave him at the end of his year in office as president of a society important to him. She told him she would continue to live with him until this period ended, to give him time to adjust, and for nine or ten months continued to accompany him to his society's functions as she had done before.

One of the most difficult tasks when two people separate and divorce is to loosen the emotional bonds with your partner. Though physically living apart, it can take a long time to establish emotionally separate lives. The important transition may not be complete at a time when you begin to live with someone else. It is 'work' which still needs to be done because the bonds linger and cannot simply be cut without repercussions. This enables you to separate in the true sense and continue to build, with your separated partner and children, a very different long-term relationship.

The subtle dependencies which built up in the relationship you have left now have to be let go, even though the pattern of contact with the partner after separation varies considerably. Small things can assume greater importance than they would otherwise. To take one example, in all relationships there is a reciprocal set of household tasks divided between both partners: shopping, cooking, gardening, fixing the car and so on. Separation involves breaking this particular pattern and perhaps learning how to do some jobs you did not attempt before. This is often a gradual process which can take several years. One way of helping to make this change, which some people adopt, is to pick the right moment to ask their partner how to do a particular job, or alternatively offer to show them, or a friend may help. This is all part of establishing a post-separation relationship. One woman, on leaving, attached notes to various kitchen gadgets to aid a particularly impractical husband. If you don't know how to change a fuse or use a washing machine, you could find out.

However, there is a danger in asking for help from your partner all the time or in offering too much to them. Because money is usually short at this time it is tempting to have too much contact, which could be misinterpreted; it may be a double message that you don't really want to let the relationship go. Some people will take any attempt to help as a sign that you will go back. Continuing ties of this kind make it difficult to free yourself finally at an emotional level. The kind of help you give or ask for, if it continues, needs to reach the point where it is on a friendly basis, as with any other friend, and without emotional overtones.

There is yet another reason why these ties have to be released. Unless this change is completed they will colour and interfere with any new relationship. Without gaining a measure of your separateness and identity you may relive the old relationship within new ones and so undermine them.

The experience of break-up that some people go through affects them so deeply that the emotional pain can become a kind of paralysis. Their feelings may be so badly affected that they find it almost impossible to trust anyone afterwards and they may withdraw into themselves and shut off new relationships. Regret and bitterness are normal after such an experience, especially if you are now in difficult circumstances as a result. A period of withdrawal can allow a healing process to occur. The danger is that regret, bitterness and withdrawal can harden into permanent attitudes of distrust which undermine every aspect of your life. However, the 'new start' that people often want after a very bad experience can come from within the experience itself.

Every marriage crisis emphasises fundamental differences between the two partners involved. Sometimes these take the form of marked personality traits in one or both which become exaggerated to the extent that they are the crucial factor in the continuance of the relationship. In many cases they progressively undermine the relationship until its inevitable collapse. These personality problems are emotionally very draining and can be extremely difficult to deal with. This is because they make it hard for the relationship to function from day to day and, secondly, because they are a product of the particular personalities of both people. These problems are complex and include, for example, explosive temper, constant deceit and extreme selfishness, heavy drinking, gambling, drug addiction, violence, promiscuity and combinations of these behaviour patterns. The deep anguish and perhaps fear these problems generate can make the other partner feel helpless and powerless. These problems can be so deep-seated that you may require professional help to find ways to resolve them. The danger is to leave things too long. However, if you are suffering, or have suffered, we want to point to some ways of coping which, we believe, can help to ease you through this phase.

First, part of the build-up to these problems is that when you were attracted to your partner originally, you were also drawn at an unconscious level to some of their unseen or unattractive qualities. They made a similar 'choice'. The powerful, even obsessive, attraction which two people feel for each other at first, and sometimes continue to feel, can obscure the necessary adjustments which have to be made to put the relationship on a more reliable basis – or to 'withdraw the projection' to use the psychological term.

It may take a very traumatic experience to shatter the illusion. A woman who found herself in a violent marriage said she genuinely believed that things would return to normal and they would live happily ever after. 'The point was that I still loved and cared for him desperately. It wasn't until I wound up in hospital for three weeks I realised I was wrong.'

Violence in marriage brings up special problems because events can reach a very dangerous stage long before one or both partners decide to make any change, or decide to leave. Violence can range from an occasional blow in anger to regular physical assault. When a relationship starts to go wrong, because men are usually stronger and more forceful than women, the aggression that is within them can turn into a behavioural pattern where blows and fights take over. Less commonly, a woman may be the more powerful partner and a similar problem can arise. Two very strong-minded partners match each other in their aggression. The actions of both the 'aggressive' and the 'passive' partners may well have their roots in childhood so that old patterns and frustrations are being played out. For both partners their energy is being expressed in a distorted way. In the case of the 'aggressive' partner, it is unchannelled and so not used constructively, while the 'passive' partner is denying their assertive qualities and so failing to stand up for themselves. What we have here is a psychological vacuum in which the 'passive' partner allows the 'aggressive' one to act out their innate assertive qualities.

Continuing violence at some point forces a choice as to whether to live with it, with the obvious physical risks, or to try to change the situation by leaving or by looking for a way to improve matters. You may already have decided you must leave out of sheer desperation and not knowing what else to do. However, violence can stem from a gradual change of a personality, leading to illness. Small changes in behaviour in the relationship can build up, hardly noticed, to the point that something has to be done. The sensible first step is to establish that there is no illness, hereditary or otherwise, behind the outbursts. There is a whole range of conditions from hormonal imbalance to more rare diseases affecting the brain which can cause irrational and violent behaviour although it is more likely to result from personality differences. It is a harrowing and frightening experience to live with someone acting like this to the extent that you do not know what they may say or do next. It is also very hard to know what to do to alter the situation, especially if you do not want to admit to other people that you are being assaulted. You may become so desperate at this stage that you consider calling the police, or a neighbour may do so.

The police in the UK have set up special units that women suffering violence (it is usually women) can turn to for help. They offer a sympathetic approach, with women officers available to speak to if you do not want to talk to a man. Information from these officers can help clarify your options: for example, whether to seek safety in a refuge, or a court order against your partner.

Here are some further steps you can take. First, if you have an understanding relative within your own family, sharing the problem with them might produce a way of dealing with it. One result could be that you discover some relevant, perhaps upsetting, information about your partner's background which you ought to know. For example, some people keep a previous relationship or traumatic experience as a closed book in their life. This is often a key to their present behaviour and can help you to understand it better. Some people have a special relationship with a particular relative who can talk frankly to them where a marriage partner may be unable to. This in itself may not solve anything but can provide some support where a partner is behaving unreasonably.

If your partner accepts that illness may lie behind their behaviour he or she may see their doctor. More likely they will not admit that they need help and their own state of mind often makes it impossible for them to recognise their problem. They might acknowledge that something is wrong but need persuading to seek help. At this point they could agree to go with you to see a doctor. If they refuse you could talk to the doctor yourself. In the very worst case your doctor may feel it necessary to commit your partner for treatment.

Where it is obvious that your partner is simply behaving badly and not taking responsibility for their actions, you must attempt to put this across to them. Many people will not face up to this side of themselves while few of those involved with them have the experience to deal with this situation. If your violent partner feels sorry afterwards and regrets what has happened you may be able to use this opportunity to persuade them to talk to someone about their behaviour, whether a doctor, counsellor or minister. Realistically, they may refuse to see anybody and even if they do, may refuse to look into their part of the problem. Some violent people will not discuss anything and here you must decide for yourself the limits of behaviour you are prepared to tolerate. How you spell this out is something only you can decide. A strong statement may produce little response, some communication may open up, or it may result in more violence. But tread carefully. An ultimatum made hastily can create more difficulties.

In the extreme, if the physical danger becomes too great to endure any longer, you may simply have to pack your bags and go. It is the act of doing what you probably realised has been necessary for a long time. Even this needs to be thought out so that legal problems can be anticipated, and a visit to a lawyer first is a wise precaution. If you are a woman and there is nowhere else to go, a women's refuge – if available – will take you and your children for a period and provide support while you make new plans. Let a few friends and relatives that you trust know where you are.

Another approach in coping with violence is to consider your own behaviour. Many of us learn ways of expressing ourselves which unconsciously signal things to others we do not intend. This can be both through what is said and our 'body language'. The tone of voice and even the gestures you use could be producing angry reactions from your partner. This can even start from a single careless remark during conversation. Someone who is hypersensitive to any apparent criticism can react to almost anything you say and treat even an innocent remark as a personal attack. In an argument blind rage can be provoked in someone by dragging up old grievances instead of sticking to the point at issue. Provocative statements, or sarcastic remarks which are intended to wound and destroy a person's self-esteem, can have the same effect.

We are not always aware of the effect of our words, or manner, on others and may be provocative without realising it. Much depends on the person we are talking to and even a mild person can be provoked eventually. Try to understand how your partner experiences your remarks and see if you need to modify your approach. You may need to ask directly sometimes to find this out.

A marked difference in the strength of two personalities may itself contribute to a violent relationship. In this case the violent person may be preying on a weak and unassertive partner. The mild person who would do anything to avoid a scene is, we suggest, not putting any limits on their partner's behaviour from the very beginning. Their own powers of assertion remain unused while allowing their aggressive partner at the opposite end of the scale to do as they wish. In this way it can be said that the victim of the violence unconsciously attracts it. This interaction of opposites is bound to continue unless some change takes place. This usually demands that the passive partner starts to assert herself (or himself) to gain a better balanced relationship. In practice, perhaps, the only way that she (or he) can safely assert herself (himself) at this stage is to leave the relationship and this very act may be what the situation demands.

It may be hard to accept that a violent partner cannot change but by trying to adjust your own attitude to take some control you start to resolve the problem at another level. For some women in this position, to leave such a relationship can be the first really assertive act in their lives. Kaleghl Quinn (1983), writing about self-preservation for women, points out that those who have inner strength and a feeling of self-worth give off a sense of harmony and so minimise their chances of becoming the victim of a street attack, while those who don't are liable to attack. It seems likely that the same mechanism is at work in marriage: that a woman who is confident and assertive is unlikely to meet violence from her partner while the unassertive woman with unexpressed drive may attract one with violent tendencies that are acted out.

An attack in the street and violence in the home can be seen as close parallels, and staying in a violent marriage as in part a passive choice. As Kaleghl Quinn says, women feel very reluctant to abandon the passive female role, even to the extent of feeling sorry for the man who attacks them. She points out that women absorb the general idea that they are 'not important enough to have the *right* to be angry' about the way they are treated.

Anger is part of the normal range of emotions and it is necessary to get in touch with your anger to make any changes. Most of the same things can be said about the man who is dominated and abused by his wife. A lack of any real assertion only invites the completely opposite attitude to emerge in a partner.

A relationship in which one partner has a serious drink or drugs problem raises intense difficulties. Where do you finally draw the line and take active steps to re-establish or sever the relationship? How do you come to terms with leaving the person you love? These are difficult questions to answer. A person who has been taken over by compulsive behaviour of this kind has lost not only their sense of themselves but also most of their ability to function within the relationship. Further, the behaviour itself dominates it.

Because this involves both partners or the whole family, the very difficulties this raises can mask the underlying personality blocks within the individual concerned. Identity problems, attention-seeking, the desire to escape from a harsh world, and other factors are among the possible causes of this behaviour pattern. However, these real causes may never emerge or be uncovered in the course of any treatment, so that the individual's partner remains enmeshed in a twofold trap. There are practical difficulties and emotional draining that go with living with someone who may have the needs of a child. Further, there is the unconscious attachment between the two partners in which the caring and compassion of one is exploited by the other. This unequal relationship is closer to that of a parent and child than two adults in a mature partnership.

The love which the 'parent' partner has for the 'child' holds them as the victim of the situation because to consider doing less for them, or want to abandon them, immediately raises feelings of guilt. This perpetuates the situation. The caring here is all one way but caring also means caring for yourself. By doing too much for your partner you deny them the necessary space to take responsibility for caring for themselves.

Appalling demands of this kind are easy to discuss when they occur in other people's relationships, but for a person living through this experience the choices look bleak. The impossibility of being able to do anything which improves matters is depressing and very up-setting. The sense of helplessness only reinforces these feelings so that the spiral always seems to lead downwards. The urge to leave can be overwhelming yet seem wrong. Years of conditioning hold us in our role as the 'good' wife or husband, fearing disapproval by parents or friends, or simply thinking 'I couldn't do such a thing'. Even set ideas about the idea of 'failure' in marriage make it hard to look beyond the guilt feelings.

However, an extreme situation of the kind we have discussed demands that you face it, become aware of the options, and treat them as choices you can make. To do this will involve stating for yourself and then to your partner what you need, which requires assertion, courage and tact. Remember, any decisions you make or fail to make affect the lives of children and others who may have no power to make such decisions for themselves. Caring for oneself is as important as caring for others because it involves taking responsibility for your own life and the lives of those you love. It can be part of a process of self-discovery to realise gradually that you may be pouring enormous concern and energy into a bottomless pit.

This leaves you very little choice but to make some very definite decisions. The more difficult a person becomes, the harder it is to reach any agreement with them. With some people you simply cannot get through to them. Or it may be that you have both reached a complete impasse. It is only when this is acknowledged that you can begin to shed the false hopes, and the pointless making up, and plan for your own and your children's future. For example, you can put to your partner some conditions that, if met, will enable the relationship to function. At the same time you can make it clear that without this you plan to leave the relationship, either temporarily or permanently. Such an ultimatum may be a considerable shock to your partner, or they may take it is as an idle threat, especially if such 'conditions' have been made before. This time you must not go back on your resolve but do be prepared for emotional upsets which may follow.

Determination of this kind can arouse a number of reactions in a partner. Their behaviour may worsen or they may be resigned to your decision but it is extremely difficult to predict which way events will go. They should at least know where they now stand and thus you will too; this is in itself a step forward that takes off some of the pressure. One husband who told his partner firmly, after many violent arguments, that he was moving out for good, found at first he was not believed. When it became obvious that he meant it the atmosphere cleared and the decision became accepted. By the time he left three months later both were able to discuss calmly the arrangements that needed to be made.

This setting of definite limits to your partner's behaviour, and perhaps your own, is the crucial issue. It is a matter of cutting through preconceived attitudes and reaching the essentials of the relationship. Acting in this spirit is a way of gaining strength to move on, rebuild your life and avoid the trap of being a victim of this relationship and perhaps any that follow.

Many of the suggestions we have made in this chapter demand consideration, flexibility and concern for other people's feelings. This is not easy to achieve, particularly at a time when your own feelings may be confused. Yet there is a balance which can be reached which creates a positive pattern for your life in the years ahead. Others have achieved it – so can you.

CHAPTER SIX

Professionals

The legal process of divorce works rather like a conveyor belt, picking up petitioners and applicants at one end and dropping them off at the other, with a divorce decree and related court orders, but not necessarily any feeling of resolution

(Parkinson, 1994)

In most relationship crises, a point is reached where the issues are no longer contained within the circle of home, family and friends, but involve professional people and agencies. This is a particularly sensitive and painful period since you may have to talk about very personal aspects of your life to outsiders. Over a period these may include a lawyer, doctor, counsellor, mediator, financial adviser, and extend to your church minister or priest, and social agencies such as that for child financial support.

New divorce laws have been introduced in countries around the world to support couples who end their marriage, with safeguards for the well-being of children. In America, divorce laws vary between states; each state has no-fault divorce, either as the only ground or in addition to grounds such as adultery and cruelty. Australia, New Zealand and Sweden all have no-fault divorce: in Australia, for example, 12 months after beginning proceedings. America, Australia and New Zealand each explicitly recognises the need for both parents' continuing involvement with their children by encouraging agreed arrangements set out in a parenting plan. These plans are becoming recognised by the courts.

The United Kingdom replaces its longstanding fault-based divorce system with no-fault divorce from 1998, following the passing of the

Family Law Bill in 1996. As in other countries, counselling and mediation are now encouraged to help couples save their relationship if possible, or disengage without lasting bitterness.

The aim is to take the blame out of marriage breakdown and 'ensure the maintenance of the child's relationship with each of its parents'. Ireland's historic vote in November 1995 to allow divorce and remarriage is a further recognition of the need to provide the means for people to reach decisions about their lives.

Laws aimed at safeguarding the welfare of children have been prompted by moves such as the declaration of the United Nations Convention on the Rights of the Child, in 1989. The European Court of Human Rights also influences legislation in Europe affecting the family. In the UK, the Children Act 1989 declares that the welfare of children is 'a paramount consideration', together with the importance of continuing parental responsibility. In Australia the Family Law Reform Act of 1996 also encourages parents to agree matters relating to children.

These developments strongly influence the way professionals go about their work with clients. They are the framework used in deciding such matters as hearing children's views, reaching financial decisions, dividing property and how you both – if you are parents – make arrangements for your children.

When and how you meet the various professionals is a keynote to the way a relationship crisis, or divorce, is handled, and while for many couples events become random and largely out of their control, it does not have to be this way. For example, before initiating a course of action which could be final, consider the fact that, as one group of researchers said, 'In confronting professionals, couples with problems are often asking for permission to express their individual needs' (McAllister *et al.*, 1991).

This can be done in different ways:

> Linda was devastated when John told her he had been having an affair and was going to leave. She became desperate when he moved in with his girlfriend. Friends and family support did not help and she went to her doctor who prescribed antidepressants. These were of little comfort. In the depths of unhappiness Linda rang the Samaritans a number of times over the next few months until she eventually found herself on a more even keel.

In contrast:

> Margaret and Dick had been getting on badly for some time
> when Dick left suddenly after a huge row. Margaret, extremely
> upset and in a state of emotional shock, had to cope with their
> three children. A neighbour suggested that she and Dick could
> try getting help with their problems at a family counselling
> agency. Dick was almost contemptuous at first when Margaret
> asked if he would go, but eventually agreed. Though living apart,
> they went to weekly sessions at the agency for more than a year,
> working on their problems together with two counsellors.
>
> They went on to mediation and divorced eventually, but in
> the process came to respect each other more as individuals and
> learned much about themselves. A further benefit was that
> there was no break in the contact between Dick and his children
> who grew up with the support of both parents.

In the first example, professional people became involved only as
a desperate last resort. The second couple were able to make a clear
decision to get help to try to sort things out. This reduced the upset
of their separation.

There cannot be a prescribed route or method which every couple
should follow to handle their difficulties. This chapter is devoted to
the idea that as well as the essential contact with people such as
lawyers, there is a wider range of professional help available. At any
stage of a break-up, and afterwards, access to this help can give you
the knowledge and necessary strength to meet the issues, as they
appear, in a positive way.

We offer information and ideas for a problem-solving approach –
whether in advance of a break-up, during this period, or later – which
is likely to produce benefits. This should be true whether or not your
partner is co-operating, and regardless of whether you are on good
terms with them or not speaking. At the same time, you may need to
work on some emotional issues, particularly anger or a sense of loss,
which can create a barrier to finding solutions. A different approach
could help communication.

Divorce, if it happens, is a legal process but an 'emotional divorce',
with its necessary stages, has to take place too before you can move
on. The outcome, if you use the professionals wisely, is that you will
develop skills to work constructively through this experience.

Doctors and your health

Doctors often know that there are difficulties in a marriage even before a couple, or their families, acknowledge it themselves. This is because doctors see many patients with complaints such as anxiety or depression, migraine and skin disorders, which they know from experience are often psychosomatic in origin – symptoms of unhappiness and not pathological disease. Indeed, Relate, the relationships counselling agency, says that 30 per cent of its clients are referred by their doctor.

There is an increasing awareness among doctors that physical and emotional conditions have to be treated very much as a part of a patient's total health picture; so they may take extra time to try to reach the root of the problem if the patient is receptive. How should you approach your doctor and what should you expect?

It is as much a part of the doctor's job to discover whether there are emotional problems to be 'treated' as it is to diagnose physical disorders. He or she can be a helpful first person to talk to if you find your relationship has run into difficulty in a way that is affecting your well-being.

Unfortunately, various factors work against this whole-person approach in many practices. Because the emphasis in medical training is on a physical cause for illness, many doctors are not taught that relationship problems (and indeed other types of problems) can manifest themselves in the form of an illness. Second, family doctors often are very busy, and one way they cope with the system is by holding short consultations and relying on prescriptions for drugs as the major 'cure'.

You may go to your doctor with a specific physical complaint that could have been troubling you for some time, or a sexual problem such as lack of desire, impotence or vaginismus. Doctors are more aware of the links between emotional or sexual problems and their effects on health when these are tied in with a relationship problem. They are encouraged, for example, to ask about a patient's sexual relationship as part of the whole history where this is relevant.

If you feel that your complaint is linked to your relationship, try raising the subject to see what he or she suggests. They may be willing to talk then, or make a later appointment to see you when there is more time, or suggest seeing a counsellor attached to the practice, or a relationship counsellor elsewhere. Your doctor might offer to speak to your partner, either alone or with you both together.

Most of us are brought up to expect the doctor to take our burdens from us by giving medication to solve our problems. In an extreme situation, pills can be a useful part of the total help offered and may be prescribed for a short period. Beware of accepting them for an indefinite time, especially if your problems have not been brought out fully into the open.

The attitude of your doctor is also important. Because of his or her own values, they might make moral judgements about you, or your situation, which you find upsetting and do not help. Most doctors do not have counselling skills; if you feel that you are not being listened to, or being given sufficient help, you should certainly consider seeking a second opinion. You could try a different doctor in the practice, or see one who has been recommended.

You may be referred to, or decide to see, a complementary practitioner such as a homeopath, acupuncturist, or a 'hands-on' therapist, for example an osteopath, who may pick up the underlying concerns behind your symptoms. This can come about because they take a very detailed history and examination and generally spend time giving treatment. Another factor is that these practitioners are closely tuned into their clients' body–mind interactions. They may be able to provide support through a difficult period by aiding your state of mind or working on the body, with a corresponding benefit for your emotions.

Clergy and the churches

The clergy fall into a similar category to doctors. Without having to put up a notice on their door saying 'Marriage Guidance', they often find themselves approached by people for help with their relationship problems. Practising Christians or Jews are naturally likely to think of talking to their local minister, priest or rabbi. Indeed, he or she may be the one person whom, if you have strong beliefs, are diffident, or embarrassed, you would trust in such circumstances.

Pastors can be remarkably sympathetic, with a wisdom that comes from dealing with conflicts of the heart and mind. Like the best doctors, some have great empathy – a gift for understanding what a person is going through. Many have an openness and awareness of human nature which enables them to offer much compassion to someone who is upset or in a marriage dilemma. In spite of difficulties of doctrine, these individuals can give you a sense of guidance which helps you to find your own personal way forward.

The different faiths have a range of attitudes to separation and divorce, ranging from support, through toleration, to outright condemnation. And within each faith individual priests empathise and do give great support, with the ability to listen.

If you are Asian, you may want to look first for advice within the family. This could depend on whether you feel that family pressures, rather than the relationship itself, are at the heart of the problem. Here, you will need to feel that there is someone you can trust who respects confidences and your value system, especially if it is progressive rather than traditional.

An Asian priest from your own religion – whether Hindu, Muslim, Sikh or from a different faith – could provide a listening ear. And it should help to be able to discuss emotional problems in your first language.

Judgemental attitudes within the clergy are a reflection of the views of the faiths, which are struggling to reconcile their traditional teachings with the facts of modern life, including the break-up of marriages among the clergy themselves.

For many churchgoers, there is a painful gap between the church's teaching and their own experience. One church support group for divorced Christians talked about 'the need to express "unacceptable" feelings of bitterness, hatred, unforgiving anger, jealousy, possessiveness and self-preservation.' Behind this lay a strong sense of not being accepted in God's church. This group articulated a common concern, saying: 'There is a confusion between the aspiration to an ideal and a compassionate response to the reality of people's lives.'

Whether you would want to approach a priest about your marriage difficulties is likely to depend on the strength of your religious convictions. Indeed, such convictions may make you feel ashamed or guilty about airing the subject anyway, especially in a small community. Whether deeply committed or not, you may go through agonies of guilt about a marital indiscretion or the idea of divorce, while a practising communicant may find the burden intolerable. You may feel that a lifetime's vow to live with someone is a commitment that cannot be broken, but equally you feel it cannot continue. Your beliefs may tell you there is no alternative but to stay. Yet Monica Furlong (1981) has written: 'What is rarely suggested is that it may be an act of heroism and integrity to end a marriage that has become destructive, to get up and leave, perhaps at great personal cost.'

One answer, we suggest, is to try not to grapple with too many absolutes at once. Initially, it is better to test the water – to accept the fact honestly that you are in a kind of limbo about your marriage and you have to find the next step for yourself. One churchgoer said: 'I felt I had to stay in the marriage – keep it respectable for everyone else's benefit.' It can help to share your feelings with a sympathetic person, or a counsellor, who will not judge. It is not for you to judge either at this stage.

What will be helpful is more information about the options on divorce, perhaps helped by professional counselling, which is provided by both religious and non-religious organisations. Most of all, you will need time to work through conflicting feelings. This period could take several months and more since you need to reflect before taking any decision. One problem here is a risk of identifying too strongly with your own beliefs and opinions. They may be too narrow to deal with the dilemma now facing you. If your inner feelings point towards a separation or divorce, this need not deny a continuing concern for your partner's welfare.

Anything you now feel or do could be hindered by others' judgements of what is 'right' or 'wrong'. What is important is that you are open and honest with yourself and others. You have the right to seek improvement in your life.

The sanctity of marriage is a fundamental concept but consider that change does occur in life and this may force a person to examine whether a partnership must change with it. There are priests and others attached to churches for whom this approach is too threatening, perhaps touching personal insecurities behind their certainties. Intimate areas of relationships may be difficult for some clergy. Some lack the emotional maturity or are otherwise ill-equipped to help. Like family doctors, most are not trained counsellors and may be unable to maintain the boundaries required for handling sensitive relationship problems. Furthermore, counsellors only tend to see people they do not know personally or socially.

Some clergy hold closed attitudes. To raise your doubts in the first instance with someone who finds safety in dogmatic assertions that leave little room for the wider realities of life could divert your efforts to find a solution. This might create a situation where you are effectively discouraged from working through your feelings. In this event, rather than give up look further afield to encompass a wider view. There are always other approaches to consider.

Counselling

In facing your particular problems, you have to ask yourself some difficult questions. Do I want to improve the relationship, or is it beyond repair? Is it the relationship, or is it me? Am I being irresponsible in wanting to leave my partner? Is there an alternative? Do I want him/her to return? Can I ever forgive them? Is boredom all there is?

Such questions raise what we really want from life and the nature of our personalities, as we have explored in earlier chapters, and this takes us to the services offered by counsellors.

Counselling offers the chance to explore, with a trained listener, the options at a critical time: when the old ways of doing things seem not to work any more, or when a significant life event occurs such as marriage breakdown, bereavement or redundancy. One professional in the field offers this definition: 'Counselling is about talking through how to cope with life events – anything else is therapy.'

Counselling provides a framework in which you can express hurt, accept and explore your feelings, seek insights and perspectives to guide decisions and move forward. Do not expect direct advice. You may feel you want to be told what to do, but this is no part of counselling. Clients are left to make their own judgements and decisions because it is recognised that giving advice does not provide a solution.

Relationship counselling can involve a couple, or one partner only, seeing one counsellor. Another approach is to have two counsellors, of the same sex or male and female, working together with both partners. This has the advantage that each partner is 'represented' and avoids the possibility of one partner feeling that a single counsellor is taking sides.

Psychosexual counselling may be of help if there are problems with love-making. These may be linked to other aspects of the relationship.

Counsellors come from different backgrounds and can draw on their life experience; look for those who are trained and accredited by recognised counselling agencies. Their skills include an understanding of interpersonal conflict, and accepting each individual and their values.

There are rarely instant answers. One or two sessions could be enough, or they may continue for some weeks or months. Each lasts for about an hour. It can take time because new ways of coping or a profound change of view are unlikely to materialise overnight. The habits and thought patterns of a lifetime do not yield easily to ideas of change, even necessary change; the process requires patience on the part of both client and counsellor.

If you want your partner to go with you, to be counselled as a couple, be prepared for different responses. They may go regularly or drop out. Counselling is equally valuable for one partner who goes alone since it provides insights and strengthens self-belief, leading to solutions.

Sometimes counselling takes the form of helping people to cope with a change in lifestyle, or view of life, which has caused a rift. These can include difficulties brought about by normal life events such as the birth of a child or family pressures. Or two people could be living as strangers because of a communication breakdown; or there might be a shift in a couple's sexual relationship. At other times, counselling can help to find the most positive meaning and way forward after a crisis.

The sessions can help you sift through the issues rather than make a snap decision you might regret later. Counselling can lead to an improvement in your relationship and allows for the possibility of reconciliation if it is in a very bad state. If the relationship cannot be saved, the sessions provide the 'space' to achieve the all-important emotional separation when legal and practical steps have to be taken.

John was urged by his lawyer to seek counselling when he and Vikki decided to divorce. Vikki had admitted that she had been having an affair for two years. John says: 'For the first few sessions, I kept saying, "Vikki did this", "Vikki did that", "Vikki did so-and-so". But I didn't talk about myself. Eventually I got round to discussing things that had not been right between us which I hadn't wanted to look at, and ways in which I had contributed to the situation.'

Counselling is widely available in the UK through national organisations such as Relate and the British Association of Counselling, and most countries have equivalent organisations (see the addresses at the back of the book). Some organisations provide counselling for those with particular beliefs, for example, people of the Catholic and Jewish faiths, although these are not necessarily limited to people of certain faiths. There are also a small number of counselling and caring agencies provided by and for ethnic minorities.

Counselling organisations usually charge a fee, or ask for a contribution you can afford. At some it is free. You can find counsellors through other agencies: via the court, in doctors' surgeries, or at the workplace in large organisations. You may find that you have to wait for an appointment, but this varies from one organisation to another.

It is OK to ask for help with your relationship. Many people are reluctant to seek help and go only when in crisis, making it more difficult than it need be to find solutions. Whatever the outcome, it is likely that you will gain a greater understanding of what is happening in your life at this time – an understanding you might not have gained otherwise.

Psychotherapy

For any crisis in life, support of some kind is needed, whether it is just to be touched or held, be given a place to stay, provided with a meal, or to share some understanding by talking it through. In a marriage or other intimate relationship that breaks down, one means of support which you may find you need is psychotherapy. This goes deeper and sometimes beyond the ways in which counselling may help, by exploring the personality further to create understanding and self-awareness. Psychotherapy is not necessarily required when a relationship breaks down but for some people it is a key to aspects of themselves where some beneficial change can take place.

The word psychotherapy may immediately throw up an image of classical Freudian psychoanalysis with deep probing of the mind over several years. This kind is expensive and only useful for a few. Psychotherapy is an umbrella term for a wide range of approaches also used by counsellors. One or several may be helpful to any particular person. They have in common the helping of the mind and emotions without drugs to enable people to understand themselves better. The techniques include psychosynthesis, transactional analysis, cognitive therapy, gestalt, visualisation, hypnosis, dream interpretation and group or family therapy.

Of these one increasingly used method is visualisation, in which a person is encouraged to allow his or her mind to produce an image which can be interpreted and shed light on some aspect of themselves or the situation they are in. Hypnosis is extremely useful in releasing tensions from the past and is also used to resolve personality difficulties. A therapist may help a person explore the meaning of particular dreams, which the unconscious produces as symbols to indicate attitudes of which the dreamer may be unaware. The unhelpful attitudes can be changed and the positive ones acted on. Often a client will be asked to draw a sketch of what he or she has been visualising or dreaming about and this brings further insights.

Group support or family therapy involves working with a number of people to explore their personalities and various interactions. In this way destructive patterns of individual or family behaviour can be faced and, in time, may be altered. The likelihood is that one basic approach will be offered, but some therapists are trained in several techniques and may use one or more as they feel appropriate and which the client is happy to work with.

Many therapists help their clients to consider attitudes and feelings which influence both behaviour and relationships. To do this it may be necessary to reach carefully back to adolescence or childhood to allow the client to re-experience and understand events and attitudes which still influence him or her in ways they are unaware of, then move them forward.

Time spent in psychotherapy, which some dismiss as pointless or 'selfish', can bring significant understandings of relationship difficulties, such as:

- acknowledging your own responsibility in the interaction with your partner
- allowing you to reach belief in yourself as an individual
- learning not to judge other people
- showing the value of listening
- indicating the importance of communicating and asking if you don't understand what is said to you
- opening private areas of thought that you may want to explore but cannot talk about elsewhere
- providing feedback on your attitudes to family and other relationships.

Insights gained from work of this kind may not only help in specific ways but can be a rich experience. They can enable you to re-direct your energies and concentrate on what is necessary in your life.

Most of us want to talk about ourselves in some way, and usually feel able to do so, although we may not find it easy to discuss a problem with a therapist. Though you want to go, you may find a natural reaction against revealing personal details in the first session or two. Some of us for various reasons do not want to talk about ourselves, but nevertheless it may be useful to consider a therapist. Alternatively, assertiveness training or physical exercise, for example, may be more helpful. There is a strong element of release of inner tension in both approaches, and not everyone feels the need to delve into the past, be shown insights into their state of mind, explore their dreams or go through a year or two of classical psychoanalysis. The essential element is release in some way whether it frees anxiety, depression or personal conflicts.

The concept of psychotherapy is evolving all the time. Methods which are standard practice today often began as a radical idea, and new ones are likely to evolve. Some doctors, psychologists and psychiatrists use such techniques as a part of their practice, but they are mostly provided by full-time private therapists. The idea of psychotherapy in some form and the name of someone who can help may be suggested to you by one of the professionals with whom you come in contact, such as your doctor or a counsellor. Or a friend may tell you about one.

Because it is a wide field, a therapist is best found by recommendation, but it is worth trying to check as far as possible the reputation of anyone you go to. Psychotherapy can produce emotional and physical reactions which you need to work with and go through. These can include feeling drained, bouts of crying and aching muscles. Also there are feelings of well-being and joy. If you are in therapy you need to recognise for yourself whether a particular therapist or technique is suitable and whether you are benefiting from the work. Remember it is an active process with a two-way involvement and not a passive one such as taking prescribed drugs. If you have strong doubts, a *good* professional therapist will understand these feelings and not press you to go on. He or she will allow you to continue at your own pace, stop further therapy or find another therapist. A finishing point may suggest itself or a point may be reached where they suggest that you continue the work with someone different.

Some of these ideas may be unfamiliar to you but do try to be open-minded about the subject and put aside any preconceived views you may have. To see a therapist is not a sign of weakness, nor a label of mental illness as some believe. It is a positive step that shows you are taking charge of your life and caring for yourself.

Most therapists have experienced therapy themselves and most will have faced crises in their own lives. Your therapist is essentially a catalyst for your own change and not an authority figure or an 'expert' who will tell you what to do. Some clients do try to rely heavily on their therapist, expecting them to give constant advice or carry their burdens. However, therapists are trained to watch for this and guide their clients towards what they must do for themselves. One specific danger is that people occasionally have unfortunate experiences with therapists who handle things badly. In the extreme this can lead to manipulation of a vulnerable person by a stronger one, though common sense will enable most people to steer clear of such individuals.

Don't expect quick results in the first few sessions since it may take this time to establish a rapport between you and to find out what the therapy should focus on. The outcome of the work will be worth it.

Lawyers and the law

The point at which you decide to consult a lawyer (solicitor) is a watershed in a relationship crisis. Here you are taking a significant step that can be expected to resolve the situation, whether you divorce or not. Until this time, the intention to see a lawyer, though real, remains for many people just that. The lawyer's part in the process can be a crucial one because he or she helps to set the tone of any divorce proceedings, which influences the future relationship with your partner.

The starting point, even before looking for a lawyer, is to consider what you want. Examine your feelings and state of mind as calmly as you can. You may be uncertain whether you want to divorce or not but simply need to find out where you stand. You may want to know whether a court would grant a divorce, or you just want to get things over and done with. It could be that you feel a need to sort things out after being separated for some time, or must respond to a letter from your partner's lawyer. The most important thing is to be practical. No matter what your circumstances and your feelings, you need as simple and sensible a way of going about it as you can manage, and a lawyer who will be helpful.

If you already have your own lawyer, you may want to see that person now. If you both have had the same lawyer handling your joint affairs and it seems unfair that either of you should have to find another one, it may be better for you both to instruct another lawyer. In general, it is advisable to seek someone who specialises in family law. In any case, a lawyer has to be found, sometimes quickly. But here the operative word is not 'found' but 'chosen'. You make a choice about the person who will act for you, to ensure that you are represented by someone in whom you have full confidence.

Try therefore to find out who the good family lawyers are in your area by asking friends, a community advice centre or professional person you know. It is usually assumed that when you see a lawyer, he or she automatically will act for you, but you could ask for a short initial meeting to establish whether their approach will suit you and find out how their costs are structured. Alternatively, ask for a leaflet explaining their approach, or if they have a code of practice.

At the first meeting you will be able to judge whether their manner and initial proposals are helpful. Your lawyer's attitude is as important as your own. If he or she is understanding and relaxed, businesslike and listens carefully to what you say, you are likely to get the advice you will need.

Equally, try to listen carefully to what they say; take a pen and pad with you to make notes, if this helps. At the end of the first meeting, your lawyer may well suggest particular courses of action such as writing a letter to your partner or issuing divorce proceedings. Unless this is very urgent, it is usually wise to ask for time to consider what has been discussed before giving firm instructions. It is easy to be intimidated by lawyers and be swept along on a course of action that it would be wiser to spend time reflecting on. You could ask your lawyer to let you see a draft of any letter or document proposed and this will help you to think about the options available.

A situation which may be fraught demands considerable tact and sensitivity, and it is essential that you are represented by someone who acts firmly but diplomatically, and with a good sense of timing.

The lawyer's vital function is to know your legal rights and those of your partner and any children you may have in your particular circumstances. The law is complex and changing, with many legal and financial pitfalls, and it is important to be aware of the rights that each of you has to gain a clear perspective on your position. Your lawyer's responses will vary according to what needs to be done. He or she may explain the divorce procedure, or advise some immediate action in serious circumstances such as risk to your home or threats of violence.

You may be feeling angry with your partner, hardly speaking to them and decide you are not going to concede anything. They may be in a similar mood. You both may find a lawyer prepared to write sharp, demanding letters to the other party, for a fee each time, of course. If both sides dig in their heels, the stage is set for a bitter battle which may last long after the legal proceedings are over.

This is the typical adversarial divorce we are all aware of and read about in the newspapers. However, new approaches in various parts of the world mean that many lawyers now conduct their cases differently – in a constructive way that allows a couple to resolve differences and reach a fair solution.

In the UK, family lawyers work to new Law Society guidelines incorporating a code of conduct devised by the Solicitors Family Law

Association, in a move to end the adversarial approach. The association's members see the divorce process more as a partnership between lawyer and client than clients simply being advised and represented. They act adversarially if required, but beware the confrontational lawyer: when the lawyer acts this way, or you demand it, costs can escalate and you have to live with the outcome of their work.

Under the UK legislation, for England and Wales, until 1998 one of five 'facts' must be accepted by the court so a divorce can be granted. These are: your partner has committed adultery; your partner's unreasonable behaviour; desertion by your partner for a continuous period of at least two years; you have lived apart for two years and both agree to divorce; you and your partner have lived apart for at least five years.

The new Family Law Bill, effective from 1998, aims to minimize bitterness between partners, promote continuing relationships between a couple and their children, and contain divorce costs. It allows divorce in a total time of about 13 or 19 months after the first step – attending an information meeting – has been taken and one or both partners has made a statement that the marriage has broken down. A divorce is granted after a specific timetable has been met, in this order:

Information meeting – 'Cooling-off' period (three months) – Statement of marital breakdown – Period for reflection and consideration (15 or 9 months) – Divorce order (28 days)

At the information meeting, details are provided on: the divorce process, legal advice including legal aid, the financial implications, counselling, mediation, and how children can be helped to cope. Each partner may attend the same or separate meetings.

At least three months has to elapse before divorce proceedings can be started by one partner (or both) making the statement of breakdown, with two weeks allowed for notification to the other partner.

Voluntary counselling is encouraged during the period of reflection to explore the relationship and allow an opportunity for reconciliation if the marriage can be saved; and mediation to help resolve differences. The consideration period is 15 months where there are children under the age of 16, or one of the couple requests it; or nine months in all other cases.

The court has some flexibility to vary the reflection period if the wait would be detrimental to children. Under the new rules children can be legally represented separately in certain circumstances such as where there is violence in the home.

Where there is violence, the new legislation seeks to reduce the risk of this occurring during the divorce process; and enables a third party, such as the police, to take legal action on behalf of a victim.

It also brings in pension-splitting, where an agreed proportion of one partner's pension is granted to the other at the time they divorce.

You may be feeling guilty, angry or ready to blame your partner, and this will not be removed by having a no-fault divorce. But these feelings can hinder a solution that is sensible for both of you. Your lawyer will be able explain how to seek a fair and constructive settlement and the ways this can be achieved, and what any course of action is likely to cost. He or she will probably discourage you if you want to use your partner's conduct as a weapon in financial proceedings. The court may take conduct into consideration where this relates to the welfare of children.

Under the Law Society's guidelines, lawyers are urged to 'promote co-operation between parents in decisions concerning the child, and should consider encouraging arrangements to be reached direct or through mediation.'

If your situation is heated or you are very upset, the lawyer will understand and listen to the emotional issues when you explain the background. But remember that your lawyer is there primarily to help with the legal matters, not to act as a counsellor. He or she might suggest counselling – if you remain too upset – to think or talk things through, or mediation to help you talk things through together. This is sensible because lawyers charge high hourly fees for their time. Counselling and mediation have become elements of divorce law in many countries as ways of managing upset and conflict.

For Jewish people, the question arises when divorce proceedings are begun of obtaining a *get* – a religious divorce. This is something to discuss at an early stage. Your lawyer can then ensure in correspondence with your partner (and his or her lawyer) that a *get* is agreed between you, safeguarding the status within Judaism of you and your children.

The lawyer can check as the divorce paperwork proceeds that your partner has applied for a *get* (if you are a wife) or accepts it (if you are a husband), enabling it to be mentioned in the order for the civil divorce. If there are difficulties, the lawyer can take steps to resolve them on your behalf if necessary. Once a *get* is obtained both partners are free to remarry within the religion.

There are practical ways you can help your lawyer, and therefore yourself. One is to tell him or her, factually, all they need to know. Try writing down, before the first meeting, any points you want to make. It is usually helpful also to take along a brief financial outline of your house value, loan on the house, and income levels. The more efficiently you can provide this information, the more able your lawyer will be to keep the legal costs down. He or she is acting in your interests but to do so will want to understand the full circumstances.

Unnecessary trouble can be avoided at this point. If you present a highly coloured account which leaves out something important, the first letter sent to your partner could well include distortions and untruths which set things off on the wrong foot.

One family lawyer said: 'I allow plenty of time to listen to the client's story at the first interview. This helps me to understand their concerns and find information they may not realise is important to mention. And I can pick up on factors which may be influencing their partner's behaviour.' Another said: 'I always have to pay attention to the basic requirements of the other party, because this enables settlements to be reached more easily.'

It may be painful to talk about events in the marriage but bear in mind that while what has happened is very personal, your lawyer will have heard many similar stories and will aim to maintain a factual approach and keep the discussion down to earth. There is no need to deliberately paint an unpleasant picture of your partner, or denigrate yourself, as some people do. The facts speak for themselves and the more magnified they become the less likely it is that things can be settled. An out-of-control divorce is like a forest fire – it consumes everything in its path and is expensive.

You may also be asked about your hopes for the future, so that efforts can be directed towards what you need. A lawyer explained: 'I always ask a client what, given their new circumstances, they would like to be doing in two years' time if I could wave a magic wand.'

The obvious anxiety you might have about the outcome is understandable, but try not to worry unduly. Providing support and explanations is part of the work on your behalf. One client was told: 'Let me worry for you – that's what you're paying me for. When the time comes for you to worry, I'll write and let you know.'

You can ask to see a draft of the first letter that is to be sent to your partner, to ensure it does not say anything you did not intend. Your lawyer should agree to this without question if made as a simple request, not a demand. Lawyers do not act of their own accord but on their client's instructions. There are good reasons to ask. First, to confirm the statements are correct. And second, because some lawyers' letters are too blunt by normal standards. We were told by a divorce specialist: 'I always take great care with the wording of that first letter to my client's partner because they may read it as making a threat even when it is not.'

Communication does not have to be only via lawyers. If no court order intervenes, there is nothing to stop you meeting your partner, writing letters or phoning to clarify points that need to be discussed – if one or both of you has the confidence or is prepared to try. At the same time, don't be bullied into accepting proposals you are not happy with. In this case, it is better to let your lawyer negotiate for you.

An occasional exchange of letters between two people who find difficulty in talking is a useful way to keep events stable. If there are children to consider, it can make all the difference if one person perseveres. The less willing partner may learn to understand the importance of keeping channels of communication open.

During negotiations, some lawyers make it a practice to settle queries and negotiate over the telephone directly with other lawyers. They may also go to see them in person. Sometimes they arrange a round-table meeting attended by both lawyers and their clients which can correct misunderstandings and reach an agreement. This saves time and reduces the final cost. These are methods you might ask about at the initial meeting.

Paul made a settlement offer to Rosemary through his lawyer, which she was advised was inadequate. After a series of letters passed between the two representatives, Paul could see 'that they [the lawyers] were getting into a fight'. He said: 'When

mine told me he was sure the court would regard the offer as
reasonable, I instructed him to stop writing any more letters
since the legal bills were going to cost more than was in dispute.
I explained to Rosemary what I had done, and why, and
eventually the court approved the original offer.'

Keep in touch with your lawyer so that he or she has essential
information. The aim is to achieve a settlement which is a realistic
balance of the future needs of both you and your partner, based on
accurate facts. Beware of attitudes in your relationship, or conduct
which may have led to a separation, affecting this realistic balance.

Taking care of the future also means making a will, or changing it
if you have made one. This is because, in the UK for example, a
divorce (decree absolute) automatically cancels a will already made.
In any case, your life and your alliances are changed by divorce. You
might want to ensure, say, that children are the main beneficiaries.
You may have another partner, or new family, to consider and need
to put your affairs in sufficient order to save confusion or wrangles
which could otherwise occur years later. Remember also to tell those
concerned that you have made a will, and where it is kept.

The idea of making a will gives many people an uncomfortable
feeling but treat it as 'just business', something that needs to be
done. Disputes over wills, or lack of them, can divide families for
generations; if you are getting divorced you have a responsibility to
try not to leave potential confusion behind should you die. If your
family wants to argue over what is left, and to whom, that is another
matter, but at least you have made your wishes clear.

Mediation

Mediation is becoming one of the most important steps forward in
helping couples who split up to negotiate a resolution to issues in
dispute over children, property and money, and may include the
issue of separation and divorce itself.

Typically, it comprises two to six meetings of about an hour and a
half each, where separating or divorcing couples are helped by
impartial third parties – mediators or conciliators – to reach jointly
agreed decisions instead of taking their disputes to court. Mediation
in divorce is not about helping couples get back together again,

although the possibility is not excluded. To show what is involved, we describe the background to mediation and then explain how it works.

Mediation has been described as 'assisted decision-making'. It encompasses skills that have been used for decades to help resolve industrial relations disputes and international conflict, and is used increasingly in workplace and family disagreements.

Mediation in separation and divorce began in the 1970s in the UK and the United States. Agencies offering mediation have developed in Europe, Scandinavia, North America and Australasia. In Sweden, 20 per cent of married couples who split up get help to resolve their disputes at meetings with an independent mediator in the social welfare system.

The main aims of mediation are to:

- help people achieve better communication;
- achieve a more amicable separation or divorce by working out mutual decisions rather than have court decisions imposed;
- reduce conflict and upset for children;
- reduce legal costs; and
- find ways for both to continue to function as parents after they divorce.

In most countries it is voluntary, but in three US states – California, Maine and Iowa – couples must enter mediation when they want to divorce and there are issues over children.

Mediation is a relatively new profession. It varies from country to country and within countries. In Sweden, Ireland, Quebec in Canada, and in Australia, there are government-funded services which are free. In the United States, the UK and Australia, there is a combination of public-sector and private-sector services, and charges can vary. All these services are still being developed and research continues into the most effective ways to fund, provide training and implement them.

Up to now, most mediators have come from a counselling or social work background, but lawyers specialising in family law – and other professionals – increasingly also train as mediators. In the UK, National Family Mediation trains people from a wide range of backgrounds. A lawyer-mediator may be present at the sessions, or a lawyer may be brought in to help with specific issues. In New

Zealand, either partner can ask for a court-supervised mediation conference presided over by a family court judge, which either partner's lawyer can attend. The New Zealand courts also have 'power to require attendance for counselling or mediation'.

In the UK, mediation is voluntary. Couples in England and Wales are encouraged to attend under the new divorce legislation which was enacted by parliament in 1996 to be implemented two years later. The UK has several mediation services: one for the in-court resolution of children's issues in the family court; one for out-of-court services co-ordinated by the charity National Family Mediation (NFM), with 70 centres; and the private-sector Family Mediators Association (FMA), many of whose members are lawyer-mediators.

Family court welfare officers usually work at court and have a statutory responsibility for child welfare, while independent mediators work *before* and away from the court. The service court welfare officers provide is called 'dispute resolution'.

Scotland has its own national mediation service, called Family Mediation Scotland, with about a dozen centres operating in mainland Scotland, Orkney and the Western Isles. It is fully integrated with the country's legal system and the courts have power to refer a couple for mediation. In addition, a private-sector service of lawyer-mediators has started.

In Ireland, mediation is provided by the Family Mediation Service, with two centres, funded by the Department of Equality and Law Reform, plus independent mediators. These services give help to couples under the country's judicial separation legislation, which allows family and financial arrangements to be settled following marriage breakdown, under the law Ireland has adopted allowing divorce and remarriage.

Mediation can be used to resolve a single issue – for example, which partner children are to live with and when they can see the other parent. Financial support from the UK legal aid system is usually only available for mediation of children's issues which have been referred to mediation services by lawyers.

Alternatively, mediation can be 'comprehensive' or 'all-issues' mediation, covering financial support, division of the home, property and money, and arrangements for children. Thelma Fisher of

National Family Mediation says: 'It may make divorce an easier experience for some people because they won't feel the other person is getting one over on them.'

The term 'conciliation' is now less used because it can be confused with both counselling and reconciliation. 'Reconciliation' has the aim of helping a couple achieve the outcome of staying together.

Does mediation work? Yes, for many people. It depends on the willingness of both partners to negotiate their differences, with guidance, on a reasonably equal footing. In practice, one partner may be more willing than the other initially.

The advantage is that you both retain more control than if you and your partner battle it out in the courts. Going back again and again to the court can be expensive. Entering mediation at the right time, with backup advice from lawyers, can bring a resolution that satisfies both people.

Here we give a picture of how mediation sessions work in practice. However, you should remember that this is an illustration: there is no standard format and everyone's experience in mediation is different. What is discussed is confidential – except for financial information, which is provided on an open basis: applications to the court for orders made with mutual consent require full financial disclosure to have been made.

Sessions may be conducted by one mediator or two working together. Where there are two, if possible one will be a woman and one a man to provide a gender balance. Where only one partner has approached the agency, the other will be encouraged to take part – the agency may contact them.

The initial meetings include an information-gathering exercise. The mediator will seek to clarify the issues that need to be sorted out and ensure that mediation is suitable. Lisa Parkinson, a founder member of FMA, says: 'Some couples come with readymade plans that they simply want to check through with neutral, well-informed professionals. Others come with heated disputes and no idea how to move forward.'

The mediator will take account of any factors which make it difficult, or impossible, to proceed at this time – for example, if one partner is too upset, or at risk of violence. They may suggest a short initial session separately for each of you to clarify whether mediation is suitable.

Mediators seek ways of achieving a power balance between both parties. This is to resolve inequalities, perhaps a longstanding feature of the relationship, which can interfere with the negotiating process. These could include one partner (usually the man) having complete control over money; a wife who does not know what her husband earns; where one partner is much more articulate, or tries to dominate the discussion; or where one partner is unclear about their legal rights.

Mediators occasionally work with couples where there has been violence. They create safeguards such as arranging for the partners to arrive at different times, and wait in separate rooms before sessions, and identify, in separate sessions, whether mediation is suitable. The mediator might suggest alternative steps.

The mediators take a flexible approach. They will not tell either of you what to do; they are there to help you work towards an agreement. They may suggest delaying mediation at the initial session, or later, if they feel resolution will not be reached at that time. If agreement cannot be found on some issues but is likely on others, they may continue.

Sessions are conducted in a businesslike manner, often using communication aids such as a flip chart to take you through various stages. At the first or second session of an all-issues mediation, you can expect to be asked to return next time with full information about your income and earnings. Each of you will be given a financial worksheet (budget sheet) on which to list your individual and joint assets. Any debts must be included since a way to settle them also needs to be worked out.

Expect the mediator to ask each of you to set out two budgets. One is to show your present income and expenditure, the other the income you need to live on after the joint resources of your home and other assets are divided. The information has to include everything: savings, pension, and stocks and shares as well as what you earn. The aim is to negotiate on the basis of full disclosure of all financial assets and an understanding of what each of you will need to live on under separate roofs. This exercise will show how far the resources must be stretched to do this.

The financial disclosure becomes part of the information available to the court when it approves the divorce arrangements. But everything else discussed during the mediation sessions is confidential and not admissible in court. This protection will not apply where information emerges to suggest that a serious crime may have been committed – if, say, one partner claims the other has sexually abused a child.

At the second stage, the mediators will help you both to clarify the issues and find ways to communicate what you want clearly. By reflecting back the other person's view and restating what was said, or putting it in a context that may not have occurred to you, it is surprising how a stuck issue can become more manageable.

Mediators are trained to deal with manipulative or intimidating behaviour and keep to practical matters as far as possible. While they will enable you to acknowledge your fear or anger, mediation is not the place to re-run heated arguments.

Mediators are trained to be good listeners, to manage anger and upset, and skilled at keeping things on track. They will listen to a particular disagreement once, maybe twice, then move you both back to the issue – 'getting people off the wheel', as Maura Wall Murphy of Ireland's Family Mediation Service puts it.

Because the needs of children are put at the forefront of divorce arrangements, mediators provide a forum to seek creative solutions to a number of problems. You might be asked if you both want to work out a parenting plan. The sessions emphasise the role of both parents for their children. This can help to achieve a breakthrough where a mother is not allowing the children's father to see them, perhaps because she feels it makes life easier. Fathers have equal importance to mothers in the discussion and mediation encourages them not be marginalised. Both parents are actively involved in making future living arrangements, and helped to agree the time spent by children with each parent.

When there is disagreement, mediators may draw out ideas to break the deadlock since children cannot be in two places at once. The options decided often prove more beneficial for children than the traditional Saturday or weekend visit – and serve the interests of everyone. Children may be invited to a session by the mediators to seek their views which are then taken into account. However, children will not be asked, for example, to choose which parent to live with.

The emphasis will be on looking at the options on which you and your partner will base your decisions. These can include short-term arrangements, or agreeing to try out an arrangement which could be re-negotiated later. Expect some searching questions. Do you want to stay in your present role? What do you want to do with your life? You may be encouraged during, and certainly after, mediation to consult your own lawyer before committing yourself to the terms of the proposed settlement.

Mediation encourages you to build trust, to find ways to compromise productively, arriving at a 'win–win' result rather than the 'win–lose' outcome typical of adversarial divorces. Issues may be stirred during the sessions that are upsetting. If you or your partner has had counselling, this will help.

One participant (a man) said: 'By behaving as if I am sensible and responsible, I actually became sensible and responsible . . . Because I knew they didn't want to hear us scream at one another, I didn't' (Walker *et al.*, 1994).

When the time seems right, you will be asked to make a written proposal. One local mediation service explains in its leaflet: 'The mediators will help clients to prepare a "memorandum of understanding" which is a joint statement of all that has been decided between you. It may also include issues which require further negotiation by solicitors or a decision by the court. The memorandum is not legally binding but is intended as a basis for solicitors to draw up a legally binding agreement.'

Your lawyer will confirm that the proposed settlement, including any lump sum to be paid, agreement covering income, and arrangements for children, is in your interests. Where there are children, payments agreed can be varied by the court, or child support agency if it is, or becomes, involved.

Lawyers increasingly suggest mediation, or you could raise it with them. Lawyers' attitudes vary. If you want to try it, agencies can be found through the various organisations, counsellors or in the local phone book. If possible, contact more than one agency to compare what they offer: their aims, skills, and general approach. Because services differ, and some are quite new, we believe it important to ask exactly what is being offered, to find out if it matches your need. In the UK and

New Zealand, for example, agencies are part of a uniform system; but in the US common standards are still being discussed.

Ask about training and accreditation of the agency's mediators. Is single-issue or all-issues mediation offered? Are both male and female mediators available? What expertise do they have if there are financial issues? For example, is there a lawyer-mediator for helping to resolve financial and property issues?

For those with complicated financial affairs, it may be more appropriate to have these dealt with elsewhere, by a lawyer or accountant. Check what charges are payable and budget for these. If it seems expensive, remember that a legal battle is likely to cost much more. Research has shown that couples are more strongly committed to keeping agreements they have made with the help of mediators than abiding by decisions imposed by a court – court decisions may be flouted.

Research by the Relate Centre for Family Studies in the UK (Walker *et al*, 1994) and in America has shown that mediation brings results. Joan B. Kelly, in California, says: 'When offered by experienced mediators with good conflict management skills, mediation provides a safe place for angry parents to discuss a wide range of parenting issues after separation' (Chandler, 1991). Both NFM and Family Mediation Scotland report that agreement was reached in 70 per cent or more of cases in 1994–95.

In its mediation brochure, the Family Court of Western Australia says: 'You are able to move forward and make a new life for yourself; your continuing relationship as parents is likely to work better; you may improve communication with your former partner and be better able to resolve disputes in the future.'

Should you go ahead, be prepared for a learning experience. Few of us are skilled negotiators in our everyday lives and most people can learn something about the art of listening, and about getting what they want without the other person losing. While it can be demanding and upsetting, there are lighter moments when people realise that their argument is simply ridiculous. And it can be, as one mediator puts it: 'a healing and transforming process'. Here you will find an opportunity to put problems in perspective.

Child contact centres

Child contact centres are a 'neutral ground' run by volunteers, where a parent can take a child (or children) so that the lone parent can spend time with them in supervised conditions. The aim is to help children maintain family bonds during a period when disputes between parents make it impossible to agree other visiting arrangements.

Centres can be found in a number of countries. There are networks in the UK and America, for example. In the UK, grandparents can maintain contact with their grandchildren through visits at a centre arranged under a court order where necessary.

In England, Scotland and Wales, there are 150 such meeting places affiliated to the Network of Access and Child Contact Centres, with some run by the WRVS (Women's Royal Voluntary Service). Most of the centres are in towns and cities, with a few in rural areas. In England and Wales, the majority of parents are referred to the centres by their solicitor or the Family Court Welfare Service.

If the option of using a centre has not been raised, and it seems the only way to maintain contact with your child, you might want to try it. The national network will give you the number for your nearest location.

The centres usually provide toys, play facilities and light refreshments. The visiting parent can play with or talk to the child during the visit. Typically, centres open on Saturdays; some open on other days of the week and also on public holidays. Most offer the service free, some ask for a donation towards the cost.

The volunteers are trained to help parents cope with the stresses that can be involved. The idea is for parents to use the centre for a few weeks, or months at the most, until enough trust has developed for them to make their own arrangements.

Children need a familiar face when they are in unfamiliar surroundings. When you take your child, expect to be asked to wait until your partner arrives. They will be asked to wait at the end of their visit until you return to collect the child. The centres have arrangements, such as a separate waiting room, that ensure you do not have to meet your partner if you do not wish to. If you feel you need to stay during the contact period you will be asked to wait in a separate room.

You may be able to use the centre as a handover point where, by previous arrangement, the visiting partner can collect the child, or children, take them out somewhere and return them later. You will not be able to do this, of course, if a court order specifies that the visiting parent cannot take the child off the premises.

Remember that the centres are a neutral ground. Volunteers are instructed not to get involved with your problems or take sides. They will need to know something of your circumstances; whether, for example, a court order applies. This information may be provided direct by the court or your lawyer.

You can ask to see a centre before deciding to go ahead. This will give the opportunity to find out how it works and the precautions taken to make sure visits run smoothly.

To use a contact centre may not be an ideal way to maintain family bonds, but it provides a link which for a time may be just what is needed.

Money

Strong feelings are linked with money. The way it is managed in any relationship is important because how a couple regards, and spends, money says much about the values that are important to them, and about how they value themselves. This can be an issue when a relationship is in trouble or has broken up.

If you relate your own personal value to your financial position within a relationship, particularly where your partner earns the money, anxiety or anger may take over when this changes. This can be equally true for men and women.

For many women who have come to rely on a man to manage the household finances, the problem is the power imbalance. Often this issue is not even thought about in a relationship until there are serious difficulties. At a practical level many women in mid-life lack experience in such matters as arranging a home loan, insurance and paying for car repairs because their partner has always done it.

Fiona Price, an independent financial adviser in London, says: 'Men and women know about the same when it comes to money matters. It's just that women think they know less and men think they know more.' She adds that 'the male-dominated financial world' frequently patronises women and uses jargon to keep the subject of finances surrounded by mystique.

Two people living together for some time under the same roof have joint, and therefore interlocking financial responsibilities – bank accounts, home ownership, pension payments and insurances and so on. These can prove complicated and vulnerable if the relationship unwinds. If you are not married, your rights to property and other assets will be less clear and less secure than those of married couples, unless there is already a written agreement of some kind stating ownership.

When things go wrong, to ensure your security it is necessary to gain control over the money you need to live on and the assets you have shared. If you want to leave or believe your partner might, think it through first before speaking out or taking any sudden action. It might be worth collecting factual information from advisers such as your bank manager or mortgage lender, or accountant if there are business issues.

It may be that you and your partner can discuss these things and trust each other, but your finances will be vulnerable if you are not sure what your partner will do next. If you are likely to break up, or have already done so, it is prudent to ensure that you do not get caught out by anything of which you may be unaware.

Many people continue to be honest and reliable about finances whatever happens, but others become unreliable for all kinds of reasons. Some start using money, or the home, as a weapon to pay their partner back for a 'wrong' they may or may not have committed, or to assert their autonomy. Someone with a lover will have competing priorities for their money – and another person influencing what they spend it on.

It is prudent, when there is a break-up, to get the balance right to ensure things cannot get out of hand by calmly contacting the bank and mortgage lender, giving them a brief outline of what is happening. Ask what precautions can be taken to ensure that a joint bank account cannot be 'raided', and check with credit card companies, to prevent big debts being run up for which you might be liable. Also, ensure that no plans affecting your home can be made without consulting you.

It is, of course, preferable if you can talk to your partner about maintaining a straightforward financial relationship, but essentially you have a duty to care for yourself, particularly if there is a marked imbalance in who controls the money. If you control the finances, be open to dealing with your partner fairly on money matters.

If you do not have your own separate bank account, opening one will make sure you have a place where your money should be safe. Discuss other ways to ensure you develop financial independence from your partner. Check credit arrangements available, if you need credit, but also what you will be charged. You might want to open an account at a different bank if you wish to avoid meeting your partner at the cash till. Bank managers and mortgage lenders will be more obliged to help if children's welfare is at stake, so be sure to mention it if you have children.

Talking to the bank, whether personally or calling them if you have a telephone account, is very useful. The person dealing with your account will know your circumstances if there is a problem. Where joint resources are concerned, getting the power balance right can be crucial. Here is an example:

> Joe and Elizabeth had been arguing for months and were talking of splitting up. Joe was threatening that the house had to be sold to pay their large debts. Meanwhile, he had been seeing their bank manager regularly to explain their efforts to put the account back in credit. Elizabeth had never met him. Gradually she became aware from Joe's remarks of something new: he and the (male) bank manager were getting on too well – sharing the view that it was really tough for Joe to be married to a difficult wife.
>
> Elizabeth was furious. She decided to meet the manager herself and put the record straight in no uncertain terms. Then she realised this would make her look exactly as Bill had depicted her, and focus on their disputes as the main issue. Instead, she made a few notes then went to the bank and conducted a low-key, factual meeting to discuss her security. By the end of the meeting, the manager was delighted with her level-headed approach. He readily agreed to consult her in future, and suggested steps to ensure she was not put at risk.

The bank can be helpful and sympathetic, but do not rely on it for everything. Bank personnel are under pressure these days to sell insurance policies and other financial 'products' to their customers. Therefore, however reluctantly, they may see building up a relationship as an opportunity to make a sales pitch sooner or later. It is best to be cautious if the question of taking on this kind of commitment is raised.

An independent financial adviser may be worth seeing. Financial advisers can help you draw up a budget and statement of your resources, then give advice on putting your money to best use when they fully understand your financial situation. Since matters such as the status of insurance policies and pensions depend on factors that include maturity dates, an independent view will give a better idea of what some assets are worth.

An accredited adviser has a duty to be upfront about what they can do for a client and how they are paid for their services. This will reveal whether they are truly independent. They may offer an exploratory appointment free but then charge an hourly rate for advice. By doing this they can give advice to clients without having to sell something each time. This freedom enables them to help objectively with your financial planning. Anyone who offers 'free' advice may be making their money by selling the financial products that give them the best commission.

You can check with a regulating authority to find out the accreditation an independent adviser is required to have to undertake this work. As with any other adviser, when you consult one, make your own judgement that this person listens and understands your interests.

An important aspect of settling money matters between you and your partner is to fully discuss with them how much is needed to support the children, through an intermediary such as your lawyer or in mediation if necessary. This is not only for financial reasons, it will also help to maintain children's links with both parents. If a child support agency becomes involved, this will influence the amount payable anyway, depending on its current rules.

Money can go only so far. A man may be struggling, if he has moved out, to pay the rent or mortgage on his new place as well as on the family home; a woman with children may be struggling to survive on the payments he provides. To have to live on much less money than you are used to can be hard, and more so if there is not enough left over to pay for a holiday.

To accept financial help from the state can feel hurtful and make you feel that you can't manage, but may be necessary while you find your feet. For those with higher incomes the difficulties will be perceived to be similar since it is the relative difference that is felt. In reality, nearly everyone has to plan for a lower standard of living, something lawyers and mediators recognise when they help you to rearrange your financial affairs. If you do have to support yourself, taking some kind of paid employment is preferable – for your own self-esteem – to being entirely supported by others.

Both men and women can find it a shock to be responsible for all their own financial affairs when they have been used to sharing the finances. To develop confidence and take care of these aspects, at an early stage if possible, is an important transition on the road to achieving financial independence from each other. It will ensure that your finances are in as good a shape as possible.

CHAPTER SEVEN

Children

Your children are not your children
They are the sons and daughters of Life's longing for itself.
They come through you but not from you
And though they are with you, yet they belong not to you.
You may give them your love but not your thoughts,
For they have their own thoughts.
You may house their bodies but not their souls,
For their souls dwell in the house of tomorrow which you cannot visit,
*   not even in your dreams.*
You may strive to be like them, but seek not to make them like you.
For life goes not backward nor tarries with yesterday.

Kahlil Gibran – *The Prophet*

E very child is unique, and childhood is a stage in the development of an individual who is making his or her contribution to the world from the moment they are born. Children therefore are not, as many adults believe, a sort of junior species awaiting adulthood before they need to be taken seriously. They are already leading their lives. As the psychotherapist Frances Wickes (1977) puts it: 'We live from the beginning; infancy is real life, not preparation for life.'

Of course, each child has to be guided on their own route to maturity. But even from a very young age they are individuals whose own powers of discrimination and choice must be encouraged and respected if they are to develop the true confidence which comes from within.

To a child each day is special, a new adventure with new possibilities, and they can retain this freshness about life into adulthood if they remain unhampered by their parents' problems.

Children like routine, but their openness generally enables them to welcome positive change when it comes and so they develop the experience which enables them to cope eventually with the variety and challenges of the adult world. But 'upsetting' changes in their home life can easily affect their sense of security. Whatever the changes in their life, they depend on a strong underlying stability, whether there are two parents or only one. For these reasons children find difficulties and uncertainties between their parents profoundly worrying.

Young children pick up the emotional atmosphere at home and often 'know' when something is wrong, even when nothing has been said. But they cannot easily interpret the verbal and visual clues which older children and adults might notice. This puts them at a serious disadvantage, leaving them worried and alarmed without being able to grasp the total situation.

The question, 'Daddy, why don't you sleep with Mummy any more?' or, 'Why does Daddy stay out so much?' may be the first of many worries in a child's mind. Or it may be that regular arguments in the home have created an atmosphere which has made them insecure and scared.

The many ways in which children react and suffer when their parents divorce were detailed in a close study of sixty American families over a five-year period by two child psychologists, Judith Wallerstein and Joan Kelly. They found, crucially, that children and adolescents alike experienced:

> . . . *a heightened sense of their own vulnerability. Their assurance of continued nurturance and protection, which had been implicit in the intact family, had been breached. They confronted a world which suddenly appeared to have become less reliable, less predictable and less likely, in their view, to provide for their needs and expectations. Their fears were myriad . . . but the anxiety itself was a widespread phenomenon*
>
> *(Wallerstein and Kelly, 1980).*

Children's reactions to stressful situations may not always be apparent or clear cut. Children are enormously resilient, even to the extent of accepting a parent's cruelty, but traumatic or continuing difficulties can seriously undermine their self-confidence and dull the vital spark which enables them to develop fully. One child will internalise his or her worries and hardly react when the parents are divided, and even make a concerted attempt to ignore what is happening, particularly if the parents are trying to do the same. Another may detach in a different but more positive way, by making a clear decision not to get involved, and for adolescent children this may be the only course they can manage.

Where there are several children in a family it is often the most sensitive one who will react strongly. At school, temper tantrums, sulks and withdrawal, stealing, fighting, truancy and poor progress are all signs which can stem from a child's reactions to a troubled home life. This also includes parents' unspoken feelings and resentments. Two adults who are at war with each other, even if they rarely argue openly, may find their conflict acted out for them by their children.

Children behaving in this way can be highly disruptive at home or at school, or both, making their parents perplexed and angry. But this is really reactive behaviour which mirrors the prevailing tensions.

> Matthew, by the age of six, had come to ape the bickering relationship of his parents, continually losing his temper in the same way and even abusing them with some of the same acid comments that they made to each other. Their behaviour implanted a pattern in him which continued long after they were divorced.

The 'naughty' child is bound to attract attention, but a child in similar circumstances who is not acting up may be equally affected. Children who show their emotions in a disruptive way are at least expressing them, however crudely; 'good' children who keep their feelings bottled up may be just as much in need of help, but their need may not be apparent.

Children's greatest and most constant need as they grow up is security. It is the feeling of being safe, secure and loved which creates the foundations for their ability to make loving relationships in turn. When life between their parents is going badly they need a lot of reassurance; they need to know that they are still loved, that they are secure and that somehow the world is still the same as it was yesterday.

They also need information because sooner or later in any break-up a point is reached where the situation ought to be explained to the children, and this is often much earlier than when the parents get round to it. To take no account of this concern amounts to a cover-up which breeds its own problems. Ideally, both parents should be able to decide together that they will be open and straightforward with the children when they are old enough to understand, and explain as much as necessary from then on. Often, though, this is not possible because the rift is too great, and where nothing can be agreed, it is then up to one of the parents to resolve to take the responsibility and this may well fall to you.

The right moment for explanation has to be judged and care taken in choosing the appropriate circumstances, perhaps with separate discussions for children of different ages. Ways of putting things positively are: 'I'm sorry that Daddy and I are not getting on very well but we are trying to arrange it so that we will all be happier in future.' Or, 'Mummy has said she is going very soon to live somewhere else and she wants us to try to manage without her. I am sure that we can if we try very hard.'

The words you choose are important. There is no harm in sharing your anxieties but there is no point in throwing in, for good meas-ure, anger at your partner. Save that for other adults to hear. The emphasis is on keeping things low-key and on saying no more than the child can cope with at the time. If you are feeling very upset, then try to deal with the subject when you are calm enough to do so with some control. Children are usually sympathetic towards an upset parent but your aim, above all, is to hold their confidence in the future.

There is another reason for choosing your words with care. Remember that children can innocently pass on remarks made by one person about another and any criticisms of your partner that you share with your children could reach their ears. Children are naturally communicative and are far less tactful than adults who have learned diplomacy. The risk is that you could make things worse between you and your partner and that a difficult or volatile partner might use your comments as ammunition, or be tempted to use a child as a source of information about what you are thinking and doing. This can only put enormous pressure on a child. Finally, no matter how true, any adverse criticism of your partner will force a child to take sides for the wrong reasons, and this can have widespread repercussions.

For these reasons it is unwise to discuss sensitive matters in front of the children – even obliquely – believing that what they do not understand will not concern them. Until well into their teens children have yet to learn the subtleties of language, such as the use of irony, and they may treat what they hear literally or simply remain puzzled. Their lack of understanding will worry them more and may raise doubts which last for a surprisingly long time.

> Marion, now in her forties, recalls that when she was a child of about ten, her mother had many complicated family problems which were constantly being discussed regardless of whether or not she was present. 'I couldn't understand much of what was said because I couldn't put all the words together and come up with their meaning. I felt very alarmed. It was not until years later that things dropped into place and I gradually understood. Even then it was such a relief simply to know.'

There is nothing merely cosmetic in keeping low-key anything you say to your children. The most important reason is that it provides them with the space to form their own opinions – or withhold them – so that they can find out for themselves what their feelings are. Remember that even in a divorce that is 'friendly', the emotional strain for a child may be severe. The less you can tax children about the issues involved, the better.

Most children want to be 'normal' with a Mum and a Dad, even these days when they are getting used to the fact that children often only have one parent. Everything is magnified to children because of their lack of experience, and a large part of their everyday world disappears when a parent goes. One of the key people in their life who helps them, answers questions and knows them best, is no longer around. On an emotional level, a person who has loved them since they can remember has gone, and even if that parent was very lacking in love, they will be missed, and the child will feel abandoned. On a deeper level, the child will no longer have both the masculine and feminine models – not roles – to relate to, so whole areas of experience provided by the parent who leaves are being 'stolen' from the child – a huge gap that instinctively he or she cannot fail to register.

Where there is good warning that you are likely to separate, there is every opportunity to establish attitudes which will provide as much continuity for children as can be managed. To discuss together and bring up – perhaps tentatively in the first place – the subject of what might happen and particularly how they will be cared for, provides some reassurance and gives children 'permission' to say what they feel.

It is an alarming and sad prospect that a family will not be able to stay together and it is very hard to face this when it becomes likely. Adults and children alike get very used to the comfort and familiarity of everyday life and it is usually hard to accept the implications when all this changes, except in the most desperate circumstances. But if it has to happen, much can be preserved. There is no need for all that is familiar to be thrown aside. In fact your task, as parents, is to honour as far as possible your commitment to your children. That commitment does not diminish as a result of separation and divorce; the problem is how to preserve it in the face of change.

Two partners who are still able to discuss matters can agree to continue to arrange things so that the children's lives are disrupted as little as circumstances will allow. A common practical problem is geographical; where will the partner who is moving out live, and will this be near enough for the children to visit? Some couples are able to arrange their lives so that they can continue to live comfortably in the same district, so that the children can walk or cycle the short distance between two homes. More often, though, it is not so easy. It may be necessary for the partner who moves out to take whatever accommodation they can find, even if it is miles away. Money may well dictate where they can afford to live and, for a variety of reasons, some people simply cannot cope with continuing to live in the same area as their partner after the break-up. And sometimes a man living apart from his family may take a new job a long distance away, feeling little need to stay in the same area, and this may be the reason why he loses contact with his children.

The important question is always whether the partner who leaves will be able to see the children often enough and it is here that things eventually can run remarkably smoothly if the parents have thoroughly prepared the way. Reassurance by both parents that the absent one will continue to see them regularly will go a long way to allay their fears. Children can be made to feel very much more secure if some of the usual domestic arrangements they are used to continue, such as one partner still collecting the child from school or after an after-hours activity, or a partner continuing the usual Saturday morning swimming lesson.

When separation does occur, children need to know what is going on so that they are not left with doubts or have surprise decisions sprung on them. In fact, what is to happen to the children needs to be considered from an early stage in the parents' decision to break up, not as an afterthought or part of some fixed plan. The selfish decisions which are often made, in which married couples or lovers keep long-laid plans and decisions from children until the very last minute, are evasive and sad and can only cause damage. To tell a child, as sometimes happens, that from next week they will be living with a new Dad or Mum they have never even met is little short of cruelty. Children need to know, at an appropriate moment, the answers to questions such as these:

'Where are we going to live?'
'Who are we going to live with?'
'Where will Dad/Mum be?'
'Will I be able to see Dad/Mum?'
'What will happen about my friends?'
'Who will look after the dog?'

Part of the responsibility of being a parent is to consider the answers to these questions long before the child has to ask them because this is essential to their security. In particular, it may well be a good idea for children to stay in the matrimonial home for a period at least, while their parents explore the long-term options.

Where a partner leaves suddenly with no warning there is no chance to prepare the children in advance for the changes to come. Yet either way there is an opportunity to handle the situation in the most tactful way you can devise, given some thought.

Where possible it is worth considering holding a family meeting with everyone present. Both parents can then explain to the children the details of what is to happen and answer any questions. This is useful even if one partner has already moved out and divorce proceedings are in progress. But it does rely on co-operation between the two partners and it may require fine judgement to gauge whether the meeting would be more upsetting than productive, or sabotaged by an uncooperative attitude.

> Sam, who persuaded his partner that they should hold a meeting at the family home once they had decided to divorce, is sure it helped to smooth things. 'Miriam couldn't see at first why it was necessary but she agreed and we were able to say to the children we were divorcing because it was the best way everyone could be happy in future – and that we would still love them. I also wanted the fact of divorce aired with both of us present, so they could be reassured that we were acting together and considering them too.'

Details like these can be arranged quite amicably but where the atmosphere is tense it may be necessary for you to 'take charge' and spell out the priority you feel the children should be given. It may not be what you feel like doing; indeed your partner may not want to listen. But by being assertive you can accomplish a number of things. The most important is that you are taking an initiative which establishes priorities and shows that the children's welfare is paramount. By doing so you also establish that whatever you or your partner want, it has to be within the context of least damage to the children, not at the price of their happiness.

This raises the question of whether, if the home life is not too fraught, it is worth remaining together for the sake of the children. Two people may accept that their relationship is not working but continue it nevertheless. Often, though, this is a one-sided arrangement where one partner quietly decides that they are prepared to stick things out until the children are through school. It is common for one or both partners to rationalise the situation in this way, but it is worth considering the implications: principally that this course of action resolves nothing. Whatever is at the root of the conflict remains simmering in the home during the years ahead, even and perhaps especially if both partners lead separate lives while sharing the same roof. While such an arrangement can last for many years, inevitably it is fragile. Something may occur to change it later and events then could be much more traumatic than sorting out the difficulties in the first place.

The majority of children don't naturally maintain long silences or bear grudges but if parents act in this way it poisons the atmosphere and their children start to withdraw. This is why two parents who decide openly or tacitly to stay together 'for the sake of the children' when their relationship is in a mess may be doing more harm than good, while at the same time failing to resolve their own problems.

A vital question is whether this kind of agreement is truly in the children's interests. Often it is more to preserve things as they are and spare the parents' upset than to spare the children. But even where the family is kept together in this way it can create as much trouble as it tries to prevent, as Margaret's experience shows:

> Margaret and David had gradually fallen out over a number of years until they found it hard to be polite to each other when they were both home. Sunday lunches with their two teenage children were tense and often unpleasant but as a mother Margaret felt duty-bound to stay even though she was, by now, a wife in little more than name.
>
> Eventually the suppressed anger between them made its mark on Joe, the younger child, who began missing school because he felt unable to face lessons. Soon he was taking a week or more off at a time and eventually was hardly ever at school. Margaret, meanwhile, did the rounds of school specialists with Joe, arranged for home tutors and tried hard to find out what was 'wrong' with him. In fact he was a sensitive child who had become caught up in the home's strong emotional undercurrents; he had lost the ability to learn and enjoy himself at school.

Young children often feel to blame for their parents' divorce because ideas build up in their minds which may be far from the truth. Therefore you must overcome, at this point, any reservations about giving the children a reasonably truthful account of what is going on and an explanation that things are going to change. They need reassurance that they are not responsible and this may well be important in clarifying the truth of their perception of the situation.

It is worth remembering too that older children are usually more acute than we realise and may already have perceived the truth of the situation that we deny. Wallerstein and Kelly, in their study, were surprised at the children's often realistic and sometimes sophisticated assessment of the causes of marital failure.

The final break can be planned in a variety of ways but there can be no fixed rules since every break-up is different.

> Jane agreed with her husband that she would leave, with the children, in a year's time after he had finished work on a demanding project which could not be disrupted – then moved, taking the children, straight into the house of the man she had decided to live with, whom the children had not met. This was taking a big risk but, luckily, the arrangement worked and despite this sudden introduction the children adapted well.

This strong-minded approach was unusual and it is advisable to take account of a child's feelings.

The emotional reactions of children once the break has been made cannot be predicted with certainty. The transition to a new life demands care and tact, for children can easily feel that they have no say in their own lives. Snap decisions and sudden changes of home can make them fearful and upset in ways which may not show but make them suspicious of change in the future. If children have to move it is better if they are given a chance to become familiar with their new home before moving in, with a transition period in which they can use both. This is not always possible but the important element is that they are given some time to find their feet and get used to the new arrangements.

There can be benefits in a move too. Children will miss the parent who left but usually take to a new life where there are compensations.

> Rhona moved with her two young children to a house which was much nearer the shops and their school than their home on the outskirts of town. And the children's school friends were now within easy walking distance instead of a bus ride away.

Visits to the family home by the other parent can be traumatic for a period and may even be inadvisable. But providing there is no court order which forbids contact, there is nothing to stop a couple making whatever arrangements they can devise so that the children continue to see both parents.

For example, you may not be able to cope with going into the family home or having your partner walk into the house to collect the children but this is not essential. A push on the doorbell at an agreed time and they can be met at the doorstep with their coats on, while the parent at home can keep busy with a job upstairs. In any case, children often get used to looking out of the window at the due time and eventually come to the door by themselves. This way there is no need for the parents to meet while they cannot cope with it. But in time, any half-way system such as this may well lead to a cautious, but eventually friendly, meeting on the doorstep. If the atmosphere is still too tense for this, the children can be taken to a friend or neighbour by arrangement and collected from there and later delivered back. Responsible older children can make their own way to a neighbour's or be met in a public place such as a park or shopping precinct. You will need to judge that such arrangements are safe.

These ideas may sound makeshift but they can be made to work. They do, however, require that parents set out to make continuity for the children the priority which overrides their wish to stay out of contact with each other. And they demand that agreements and arrangements made are stuck to so that children are ready and are met and returned at the agreed time. This is particularly important for younger children, who feel the most insecure; they need visits that are regular and to a timetable they can rely on. For a visiting parent to be late or change their mind and not come is very upsetting for a six-year-old who has been looking forward to it for days. Failure to be reliable and reasonably prompt alarms small children, annoys older ones and the parent at home, and can put the whole arrangement in jeopardy. If it is unavoidable that you have to change your plans to visit, always tell your partner in advance, and the children if possible. Children often get upset when there are visits. However, Brynna Kroll (1994), a specialist in family work, citing research, says distress after visits to, or by, the departed parent 'was often seen as a sign that such contact was harming the child, rather than a natural response to being reminded of a sad event'. This tempted social workers and parents to terminate contact, instead of supporting the child 'to manage the inevitable pain of the re-enactment of the parting'. Therefore, there is a need to interpret children's behaviour correctly and not allow it to be used as a reason to end contact.

The key word is reliability. As we showed in earlier chapters, it may take time, tact and persistence to prove that such arrangements for contact can work – that you can fulfil obligations despite the strain this may involve. By sticking to them as closely as possible the way is paved for more flexible arrangements at a later time; in fact as they get older children themselves become bored with the same fixed visits which make it hard to find anything new to do. Friends and hobbies become more important than parents as children grow up and this is a natural development in both divorced and non-divorced families. A visiting parent may feel rejected if a child does not want to see them on a particular day but this should not be taken personally.

The ideal, which many families reach, is that the arrangements eventually become entirely negotiable, and are partly dictated by the children themselves – the complete opposite to the stultifying contact times the courts will set for two parents still at loggerheads.

It is very difficult in practical terms to make a very cut and dried arrangement and this is, in any case, likely to conflict with the child's needs and what might suit the parents in future. A child may well take up an interest which involves spending a lot of time with the visiting parent or, conversely, may find so much to do with friends or the parent they live with that they are less interested in seeing the other parent as frequently. Again this reflects situations which have parallels in ordinary family life. A child often relates much more strongly to one parent than the other and does more things with them. We cannot emphasise strongly enough that this should be allowed for as far as possible and that fixed notions of contact every Saturday or every two weeks cut across the whole idea of children having a say in choosing how they spend their time.

Parents, until recent years, have usually regarded contact as the right to see their child, but courts, backed by law, now base their decisions on asking what is best for the child instead of what each parent wants. The law here is backing what is now seen as a child's fundamental right to know his or her parents and clearly this is a more constructive way for parents to see things too.

Contact can also be granted to grandparents and even, in some cases, to aunts and uncles. In other words, there is a recognition that the child needs to continue well-established relationships with adults other than the parents – on both sides of the family – and these should not be denied. Where a parent strongly opposes any meeting between the children and the absent parent this has a great deal to do, we believe, with an unconscious need to be with the child as well as feelings of resentment or revenge. A parent who has few interests outside the home tends to have a psychological dependence on keeping the child there. This is likely to be at the root of many battles over seeing the child though some undoubtedly are fought over the issue of which parent is the most suitable to bring up the child.

But keeping the children away from the partner has its dangers, and a child may be forced by an unaware lone parent into the emotionally damaging position of surrogate partner. In their book, Wallerstein and Kelly say that children put into this position began acting in disruptive, abusive and generally aggressive ways, often directed specifically at the mother. They 'behaved like caricatures of jealous, domineering husbands' so that the mothers felt victimised. 'Yet it was only when the mother was able to extricate herself from the victimisation and assert her adulthood that she was able to help both herself and her agitated child.'

In contrast, the parent who has some absorbing interests will usually be happy to see the child spend time with the other parent.

> Michael says: 'When Carol and I split up she was determined that I should see the children only once a fortnight. But we talked it through and she could see that for me to see more of them would help us all to arrange a divorce settlement which allowed more flexible access. Now I can also ring her a few days ahead in the school holidays and say, "Would they like to come on a train ride to the sea for the day?" and Carol is as pleased as they are.'

Michael and Carol made sure that the wording on their divorce papers reflected this flexible arrangement and we feel that this kind of settlement is a positive use of the law. In other words, by making an agreement themselves, it wasn't left to the court to force rigid 'visiting times' which at least one of them would have resented. This again shows the benefit of making the decision between you. If this is impossible, the neutral ground of mediation could help you find ways out of the impasse, as we mentioned in Chapter 6.

Under a free arrangement, once complete trust has been built up on both sides, visits can be fitted to the children's real lives in which, for example, youngsters get invitations to parties at short notice or become absorbed in a project they want to finish, in contrast to meeting the visiting parent at set times.

The whole problem of contact after a family breaks up is very difficult for many parents, even where there is little or no animosity. Resentful mothers may make it difficult for fathers to see or visit their children. This then leads to the father drifting out of the lives of his children until they regard him, gradually, as a stranger. In a survey conducted for Gingerbread, the organisation for single-parent families, some of the parents reported that they didn't mind that the parent who had left no longer saw the children, but other parents were certain that their children suffered because of the other parent's rejection of them. One person said: 'In six years there has been no contact at all. I wish there was and so do the children (aged nine, ten and twelve). There have been no presents, no cards, no contact. The children feel hurt and rejected. They have happy memories of her but unless she sees them soon I feel they will resent her for leaving them' (Gingerbread, 1982).

Another parent in the survey said: 'The children (aged eleven and twelve) often ask about their father. I don't know what to say. He lives only fifteen miles away but we haven't seen him for years. I've written to him but he doesn't reply. Perhaps he's moved. It's hard to tell the kids he's not interested.'

The most heart-rending story we heard was of a couple who divorced and the father went to live with a woman whose garden backed on to the marital home. Once he had moved in he no longer acknowledged his children playing on the other side of the fence.

As mentioned in Chapter 6, in Britain parents' responsibility for their children is now spelt out clearly by the law, to encourage both parents, when they split up, to continue to fulfil their parental obligations. The spread of child support agencies and mediation services in various countries aims to encourage this.

The emotional turmoil of having to establish a new life in difficult and perhaps distressing circumstances clearly can make people act in ways that are unfeeling or out of character. Not knowing how to act, feeling under pressure to act in certain ways, is common to many so that callous or indifferent behaviour may seem to have some justification. The urge to make a 'clean break' and cut family ties is a tempting one but can never really be advisable where children are involved. The idea of choosing to be no longer a part of a child's life has far-reaching implications. There is a big difference between the situation in which the absent parent no longer lives at home but maintains contact and one where he or she fades totally out of a child's life. Someone who, for whatever reason, never knew their father or mother, or has forgotten what they were like, may be left with a nagging void which haunts their adult life. To lack direct knowledge of a natural parent creates a large gap in a child's certainty about themselves and who they are. It also leaves him or her with an unsatisfied curiosity about what the parent was like. And it can result in a life's search to replace them – by marrying a 'father' or 'mother' figure, for example.

Parents are not necessarily in the best position to decide that their children no longer need them, or the parent who has left. Such a decision, which commonly isn't discussed, can be as much a means of avoiding more upset or be the outcome of resentment against the partner. Yet, as our examples suggest, it may be necessary to face and work through painful situations in order to avoid inflicting more distress on the children in the long term. As important, it enables two adults to continue the job of being parents.

It is a denial of this basic need to relate which creates a sense of loss that harms parents and children alike in the years to come. Nonetheless, the absent parent will sometimes get the feeling of being out of touch because their relationship with the children can rarely be the same as if they still lived with the children. This is difficult and inevitably these feelings will come and go and need to be acknowledged and accepted.

Maintaining contact for the absent parent may be a difficult business, particularly where distance or an upsetting divorce make it hard to see the children. Unfortunately, lack of regular contact can have a pendulum effect, leading to a parent whose concern for the children swings wildly from overwhelming adoration to complete indifference. Not to see the children for weeks then suddenly take them out to a restaurant and provide other treats cannot provide the balance they need. Similarly, the father who is not to be seen for months on end but then arrives with arms full of presents on Christmas Eve misses the point. In these circumstances children cannot relate to strangers, no matter how many presents they bring.

The ideal benefit you can give the children – and one which lasts them a lifetime – is eventually to reach an arrangement where the absent parent can meet the children in their own home in a friendly atmosphere. This may not be easy. The deep tensions, the mixture of guilt and anger, and the awful feeling in the pit of the stomach which may accompany many visits are horrible and upsetting. These feelings are so difficult to cope with that it is at this point many parents give up and the chance of creating a positive pattern for the children's future security slips away. You must be prepared for these upsets to reach what is important for the children; involvement with them in some of the everyday things of life which is crucial to their well-being – in non-divorced families too. Children want and need you to see little things like their new clothes or toy, or something they have made, and this is easily done in the few minutes in which a parent calls to collect them. This is a direct and incalculable benefit reached by working through the difficult period. The unpleasant feelings of meeting like this in the family home will lessen in time where parents keep the goal ahead of them, and eventually everybody feels better. But be careful not to overstay your welcome, if visiting.

The idea – and indeed approval – of the 'one-parent family' in many quarters relates to this problem of meeting amicably. The aim of independence and self-sufficiency after separation and divorce is a healthy one, for certainly a 'new start' has to be made and years of marriage or close relationship do make a lot of people too reliant on their partners. However, the label 'one-parent family' also encourages some mistaken assumptions. One parent can certainly cope admirably and develop new strengths they would otherwise not have found. But this does not require that the absent parent should no longer be in evidence because one parent cannot take the place of two. Someone bringing up children on their own has difficult practical problems to resolve but there are dangers in identifying with this as a complete lifestyle in itself. It could be only a transition period and by remaining open to the changes the family is going through, the possibility is allowed of a new 'father' or 'mother' coming into the family. To take on the whole burden and insist on bringing up the children as a one-parent family – as some embittered mothers and fathers do – is to deny them the balance two parents provide. Equally, the fact that many people find their independence only through divorcing and becoming a single parent makes its own comment on the problems of dependence in marriage. Similarly, professionals such as teachers and doctors may make assumptions about a child's difficulties which are based on preconceived ideas about one-parent families.

The problem of the absent father or mother who refuses to make contact with his or her children is a heartbreaking one, but the parent with whom the children live does not have to give up the idea that contact is lost for good.

> Sarah wrote to a national newspaper to describe the almost heroic efforts she made to spark some interest from her former husband in their two boys. For several years she sent Christmas cards from them, photographs, school reports and regular letters telling him how they were getting on. After silence for all this time, he began to reply and eventually started seeing the boys, taking them on outings and finally establishing a regular relationship with them.

All this is good reason for working persistently for some contact between a child and both parents. Where the absent parent is extremely difficult, or violent, there may be sound reasons to keep them away from the children. However, in less extreme cases, it can be argued that a child who meets the parent at least once in a while will see who and what they are and make up their own minds as they get older. If unable to meet the other parent a child may wonder themselves, as an adult, whether the parent they lived with was hopelessly biased about the other one. They are also less likely needlessly to idealise the parent they never knew.

If the relationship has deteriorated to the extent that you and your partner cannot meet without great upset, or there is a breakdown in communication over visiting arrangements, remember that you can use a contact centre, mentioned in the previous chapter, to maintain the child's relationship with the parent. For most parents it does not come to this but rearranging lives to cope with a break-up is rarely easy.

If a difficult period can be overcome so that there is no longer any upset, it makes a big contribution to the children's security for them to see that their parents can still get on together despite living apart. More than this, both parents eventually may gain respect in the child's eyes for having cared enough to maintain the links, especially if the child compares their circumstances with those of others.

One of the most difficult events to handle during the transition to a new life is important celebrations such as Christmas, Divali, Eid and Chinese New Year, which involve the family. The first Christmas after a family breaks up is often traumatic and can be a very uncomfortable time, because even parents who are on reasonable terms with each other are usually unsure whether they should have a family Christmas for the children's sake, or not. And the children are very likely to ask: 'Is Daddy (or Mummy) coming to see us?' Christmas in most people's lives is an important time when family ties take centre stage, even in families which are not particularly close.

Many separated couples with children manage to arrange at least a meal or a brief time together as a family at the first Christmas after the break-up, despite the awkwardness of the occasion. Some are able to spend Christmas Day, or part of it, together and may even need the guarded warmth that this provides. You might arrange the visit on Christmas Eve or Boxing Day instead. Tactfully handled (and with an explanation to the children in advance that it is for Christmas only), it is an excellent chance to put aside the year's difficulties and give children some of the family spirit they need. Later, new patterns for spending Christmas are created as both partners establish new lives. But it is important for children that Christmas continues to be marked by their parents acting together as far as they are capable in the circumstances. Ways of doing this include:

- Discuss and agree in good time whether the absent parent will visit.
- Make a proper arrangement about the time and duration.
- Decide jointly what presents the children should have so that they don't get presents they already have, or the same thing twice. Do this by letter if necessary.
- Tell the children what plans are being made.
- Inform other relatives of the arrangements.

Even if it is impossible for everyone to meet together, consider an arrangement where the visiting parent meets the children at a relative's or a friend's home.

Birthdays are as important to children as Christmas. Beyond the joy of the celebrations, the presents and the party, each birthday, to a child, is a turning point in the year which confirms that he or she is growing up. Children need their parents to share the occasion in some way, even a parent who rarely sees the child – it means so much. To send a card, perhaps with a message, takes little effort but it shows more than anything else that you care, no matter what the circumstances.

In the process of overcoming the upset of separation and divorce, many people try to block out thoughts of the partner who has gone. However, children need to have the opportunity to talk and allow their feelings about that parent to be exposed. So it is important to resist the urge to suppress the subject with your children, if you feel this way, even if talking about it upsets you. Allow the child's hurt feelings and accept them. And accept your own hurt feelings too.

The legal arrangements which are made for the children in the divorce settlement are a key to both partners' future relationships with them. The most common arrangement reached still is for children to live with their mother and for their father to visit. But many other, often creative, arrangements are possible by dividing children's time in various ways between two homes. The newspaper *Today* reported the example of an English couple who found houses three miles apart after they separated and agreed that their five children would stay alternate nights at each home. The children kept clothes at the two houses and saw them both as home.

> Both Paul and Georgia's homes reflect their personalities and it means the children live differently at both. House No 1, as they call their Mum's, is untidy but relaxed. Here they slob out, sprawling on sofas, trailing in mud from the garden and only occasionally getting into trouble for it. House No 2 is Dad's and here everything is tidy and organised. Everything has its place and the children like it because they know where everything is.
>
> (Today, *19 October 1995*)

The spirit of co-operation we are suggesting on major decisions can be extended to more everyday matters such as children's schooling.

For example, while it may take time to achieve, if it is possible, try to attend at least one or two of the important school functions together, such as sports day and open days, and school plays. Children love to see their parents at such events – to catch a glimpse of them from the stage or running track – and for at least one to turn up is part of normal parenting. All children need the reassurance of their interest in them, and it is equally important to children of separated or divorced parents.

Schools nowadays are very well aware of difficulties that confront such children. They usually have a pastoral care system to make sure that the general welfare of children is looked after as much as the educational aspects. Teachers often know the child's personal situation in detail and therefore can be sympathetic to any school problem. Schools learn about changed family arrangements in several ways: through the parents themselves, as an outcome of a child's difficulties, or a child may mention it him- or herself. In a school we visited, one divorce a week was brought to the attention of staff. Teachers often find a child's behaviour changes, or becomes difficult – including truancy – when their parents split up.

It is important for a school to know when there is separation or a divorce because this is a major change in circumstances, similar to other upheavals such as a house move or a death, which may affect school work or behaviour for some time. The school will also want to know what the home arrangements are so that staff know how to contact parents over notices, reports and if there is an accident. For young children, the school may need this information in order to know which parent is supposed to collect the child at the end of the day, or whether it is a parent's wish, or court order, that the other parent should not meet the child. Try to be open with the school staff about these matters; they are usually glad that both parents are still involved and will normally send information for parents to each if asked.

The pressures on children at this time may be reflected in their health. Children can become susceptible to ailments such as sore throats, stomach cramps, earache, headache and skin rashes. Illnesses such as asthma may worsen or even develop at this time. These are, in effect, an outward expression of a child's attempt to deal with the emotional problems. At the school we mentioned, the nurse told us that most of the children whose illnesses she treated were linked with parents 'who are together but in friction, or are separated'. This again strongly suggests that parents who are separated or divorced should sort out their differences as far as they can, to lift the strain off the children.

One way in which children can be helped with more serious problems is through the various social agencies. At school, if there are work or behavioural difficulties, the educational welfare officer or educational psychologist may be called in to help both school and parents find a way to maintain the child's progress. He or she can offer advice to ease the situation and may suggest one of a range of solutions.

Sometimes these problems may be too difficult for parents to handle without help. Family relationships are complex enough at the best of times but when the family is under such pressure the various inter-relationships themselves may be at the heart of the problems which are troubling the child. It is not a question of blame or feeling guilty, or of being a bad parent, but of trying to understand and change the underlying pattern which lies behind the difficulty. This complicated area of family life may be impossible to resolve without professional help such as family therapy to explore the issues.

The difficulties that children have in coping with their parents' unhappiness or break-up are often underestimated since children find it hard to deal with their feelings. As a parent you may be finding it difficult to cope with their behaviour. Your own feelings may confuse the issue. Advice or support from one of the various organisations offering help could be useful, say, to work out a parenting plan with your partner.

Linda Fisher of Relationships Australia says: 'It can be used either as a plan of parents' intentions for their children, or as a basis for orders which are enforceable in the family court. The plan also helps if one parent becomes chronically ill or dies, or where a step-parent has responsibility for your children.'

Children can survive these experiences and prosper in the life that lies ahead of them – if the right conditions are created. As Kahlil Gibran says: 'Your children are not your children . . . but you may give them your love', and this is what will help them most.

CHAPTER EIGHT

Parents, Relations, Friends and the Future

'I could tell you my adventures – beginning from this morning,' said Alice a little timidly. 'But it's no use going back to yesterday because I was a different person then'.

Lewis Carroll – *Alice's Adventures in Wonderland*

The essential meaning of 'the family' changes when you separate and divorce, so that new patterns of living have to be found. Similarly your relationship to friends will alter too, and new priorities present themselves. This chapter is about the various shifts and changes which can occur and how to cope with them. It is also about the help and opportunities which present themselves when you very much need them. At this time nearly everyone needs the lifeline that the network of family and friends provides. With a positive attitude, this period can lead to a new equilibrium, a time when you are able to strike out in the world again.

Parents are hit hard by the break-up of their children's marriages and the initial separation is often a surprise and a shock. Although older people usually have their own attitudes to marriage and the pressures involved, because of the prevalence of divorce some may understand and empathise with what you are going through. Often their reaction to the breakdown of a marriage or live-in relationship which has seemed secure is one of saying: 'They had such a lovely home together, and lovely children. I cannot understand why he (or she) wanted to leave.' This comment can be a reflection of the difficulties in communication between parents and their married son or daughter. If parents and child have been unable to discuss their feelings together, then the parents will not have the knowledge to understand, though this can be developed. Time itself can help.

Disappointment and resignation are natural and understandable reactions when parents hear about the break-up. Because the promise of a lifetime's commitment has been broken, they can easily feel responsible in some way rather than look at your particular situation as it is. They may have a sound and happy marriage themselves which has survived the difficult times and wonder, therefore, where they 'went wrong', especially if other family members have been through the same experience.

Parents do notice difficulties and ask about them at an early stage. When you have frequent contact with your parents they are more likely already to be aware of changes in the marriage. If you have a good relationship with them, these may be the first people you turn to. If they live at a distance or you rarely contact each other, then you can choose more easily the point at which you say anything – or indeed you may be asked. This could be the first time you share your upset with someone else and for some this is an important first stage in coming to terms with a breakdown.

Parents can be supportive or perplexed, or both, but the way you discuss the subject and what you say will depend very much on how you get on with them. It may be necessary to consider what they are able to handle, especially for example if a parent is ill, or rigid in their views. You may have to choose whether to say anything at all or to postpone talking to them for a long time.

Some parents, because of their attitude, find it difficult to offer you support and become angry or resort to blame as a way of coping with their feelings. This is something to try to sidestep as far as possible since it is destructive and probably merely a replay of their attitudes towards you as a child and young adult. The urge to blame can lead parents to take sides, sometimes even feeling less sympathetic to their son or daughter than to the person they married. Alternatively, parents may side with their own children and see them as blameless. You may have to cope with such attitudes, to stand up for yourself and put your own point of view.

There are good reasons for doing this. First, it is a matter of your own self-respect, and secondly, if you have children, you have a responsibility to protect them from family disagreements about the marriage which will upset and confuse them. For example, should your parents strongly disapprove of your partner and take sides by strongly criticising him or her openly in front of the children, you will need to stop this by pointing out that the children will suffer and become insecure. By appealing to their better nature as grandparents, it is possible to persuade them to be more careful about the remarks they make; it is better still to persuade them not to discuss the subject when the children are around. If this does not work and you feel the children are hearing things you do not want them to, you might have to alter the pattern of contact. One way is to try to make sure you are with the children when they meet their grandparents. Another is to limit the grandparents' contact until things change. You may be fortunate enough to have parents who give both emotional support and practical help. They may though be struggling with divided loyalties – wanting to maintain contact and support for the grandchildren in the face of anger or disappointment. They may be worried about being denied contact with their grandchildren if they criticise the behaviour of the adults involved. It helps if you can be sensitive to their feelings and also remember that they have their own lives to lead. As time goes on, you may need to negotiate a balance with them on the help they can reasonably provide.

Blame, anger and other unsympathetic reactions can stem from hidden feelings of which parents are unaware. They may be angry with themselves for having 'failed' as parents. Outbursts can also mask underlying resentment where one parent, or even both, wanted to leave their own marriage in the past but never did. A parent might even confide that they wish they had left, and this can lead to some understanding between you. Or it may simply be that they cannot understand what is going on and the reasons why.

A break-up often brings back to the parent the intimate relationship between parents and their children which was apparently left behind when the child became an adult. A man or woman facing life alone can find themselves the 'child' once more in their relationship with their parents – at the stage it was when they originally left home or married. This can happen at any time in adulthood so that even a person in their thirties or forties with children of their own may be treated as if they were a teenager or a small child. Support and practical help that parents can provide will usually be welcome, even badly needed, but it is worth being aware of the family complexities. You could find your own personality, or certain parts of it, reflected like a mirror or brought up again. If this happens, the positive side is the opportunity to become aware and gain insights into undeveloped parts of yourself and so make changes. Some people, badly hurt emotionally, return permanently to a childlike relationship with their parents, even moving back in with them for good, particularly if they have never led an independent life. If nothing else, someone who, for example, has gone straight from home into marriage, gains a lot of independence if they become separated and this is not something which should be given up in a hurry.

The relationhip you have had with your parents up to now is the starting point for talking with them about your life and what you are going to do. Many people find this is not easy for a variety of reasons, and this is particularly so where there has been a fraught relationship for some years. Even in caring families you may quickly need to establish an adult-to-adult relationship. This helps to prevent an adult–child pattern re-establishing itself, and it could prevent the relationship deteriorating. Be prepared to talk to them. Parents often have more maturity and understanding of life than we allow, even when, perhaps because of age or their own circumstances, there is little they can actually do. Their help can come in other ways. One mother in her seventies wrote a concerned but reassuring letter to a daughter leaving her marriage after twenty years saying: 'I hope you find peace of mind.'

Those who cannot turn to a parent may instead be close to an uncle, aunt, cousin or grandparent in whom they can confide. Indeed, this may be someone they have been close to since childhood. Since in many ways they provide the function of a parent, they can offer similar help but perhaps with a little more detachment. Many a family has a wise relative, perhaps an elderly uncle or aunt, who has seen much in a long life and provides a calming influence – often saying just what is needed, like the mother mentioned above.

A brother or sister, usually someone of your own age group, can provide a different kind of support. You may be fortunate that their views and values of life are broadly like yours, so they can easily sympathise. Perhaps they have gone through a similar experience themselves or, like a friend, are simply calm and steady when you are feeling otherwise. They may be sufficiently detached to point out some things you may not want to hear. This kind of honesty is not always welcome but sometimes you can learn from it.

Separation and divorce can easily lead to divisions which exclude in-laws. It can seem 'right' and 'normal' that with separation, the relationship with our partner's family should also cease. Though things may change, there is no reason, unless you have to, to cut off valid relationships that have been built up over a number of years. Indeed, it would be artificial and even hurtful to do so. Parents-in-law or other relatives on your partner's side may value your relationship with them more than you realise. One woman whose parents-in-law knew how badly their son had treated her, received their every support when he went off with someone else. Later, after a divorce, she was asked by her former husband's sister to be a godparent to the sister's new baby. Though this relationship continued, some do have to be let go and sometimes circumstances prevent you from doing otherwise. It is a difficult area in which you may need to trust your instincts.

The period during which two people separate is an opportunity to mark the transition between past and future – for both the intimate relationship and their relationships with friends. One couple, whose last year together had been cold and distant, stood in their house for the last time after their furniture had been divided and collected. They lit a candle, acknowledged their letting go of the relationship, wished each other well and blew out the candle. Two people who had talked through their separation arranged a final party at their home to say 'goodbye' to their friends as a couple. They were unsure if anyone would come but on the night 70 people arrived and the party was a great success.

New friends may emerge, longstanding ones can disappear and some relationships change in character. On top of everything else you find the need to make different adjustments among your circle of friends. It is a time when true friends show themselves and new ones help to shape your future life.

This re-mix of friends can seem very random but we are convinced it has a purpose: there must now be a profound change that reflects new areas of involvement in your life. There is no predicting what these might be but you must remain open to them. In fact, this book had its origins in a chance meeting at a party between two men who were re-establishing their social life during the period surrounding separation and divorce.

An intimate relationship under one roof can be like a time capsule because its demands take up so much of our time and most of us expect this structure to provide nearly all our emotional needs. Coupledom takes over and the friends we have must be fitted into the time that is left. For these reasons many people feel very vulnerable when they find themselves establishing social contacts as a single person once again. It can be difficult enough if you are in your twenties or early thirties and married for several years. For someone in their forties, fifties or older who has been married for twenty years, this transformation can seem overwhelming. Yet people do meet the challenge, pursuing new interests in a way not possible when social conditions were different.

As an individual you now have to create your own structure of friendships so it is no wonder that you may feel awkward and vulnerable at first: it can be like coming out of a tunnel into daylight. This vulnerability is mixed with bewilderment, even shock sometimes, when you find yourself having to revalue your existing friendships and evaluate new ones at the same time as you are re-assessing yourself. If you find yourself crying, allow it as a welcome relief.

Women are generally more adept than men at making lasting friendships at an emotional level, as well as making a deeper commitment to marriage. Most men, on the other hand, find it difficult to share their feelings and their friendships tend to be based on work or spare-time interests rather than on friendship itself. Consequently, a woman will be strongly sustained by her women friends when a marriage breaks up; a man is less likely to receive this support from his male friends. Both may find that involvement in work gives valuable support.

Most people have staunch friends who will always stand by them, but within established friendships some people fade out of your life and others become more important. Some of your friends may feel vulnerable too. The end of your relationship will provoke some unspoken thoughts in couples that you know. These can be concerns about sensitive areas of their own relationship which even result in your being rejected by them. Another reason for rejection is that they may feel embarrassed and would like to help but do not know how to. Equally, they may not be able to relate to you as a single person instead of part of a couple, or they could have taken sides and kept their sympathies for your partner.

So many of us are inclined to act in set ways and all kinds of attitudes and judgements can come into play. For example, the assumption by the female partner that a divorced woman on her own, when invited to a meal, is a threat to her relationship, is still a common one. This feeling of threat often leads to rejection of the woman which can be very hurtful. In contrast, a divorced man on his own is often thought of, again by the female partner, as someone who needs a good meal and is therefore a welcome guest. This could be a reflection of a number of aspects in the man–woman relationship stemming from old roles and assumptions. Perhaps women often sense their man has less emotional commitment to their relationship than they have, and that he might easily be tempted. There may be an unjustified assumption by both that the single woman could be interested in the man when all she really wants – like the man – is the meal and the company.

To feel yourself rejected by friends when you may be low anyway and facing other problems is painful. If you want to stay good friends don't let the opportunity pass to ask directly what is bothering them underneath. Are they judging you without knowing the full story? Are they just angry or upset for some reason? Or are you behaving in a manner likely to put them off so that they don't want your company? The answer may be simpler than you realise since they may be in a serious dilemma: do they stay friends with you, with your separated partner, or both? This raises the problem for them of whether to invite you to visit, or your ex-partner. They may even cope with the dilemma by cutting you both off for a while, or for good. If you feel yourself cut off in this way regard it, perhaps, as a necessary part of the change in your pattern of friendships. Some friends, inevitably, will drift away but others will take their place if you allow it. One of the big problems here is that the rejection of friends, added perhaps to that of your partner, can build up a pattern of expecting things to turn out badly. When you continually think this, life itself will tend to treat you accordingly. In contrast, if you expect things to turn out well they are more likely to.

New friends that you make can help you look on the bright side but you also have to look towards the bright side to make them. People are generally prepared to make the effort with someone who is going through a difficult experience provided they feel you are moving forward, however slowly. New friends can introduce you to values and areas of experience you might not have explored before. They act as catalysts. Simply through knowing them you can discover and involve yourself in interests and activities not attempted before.

Some of these friendships may be passing ones, lasting only a few weeks or months, or even a day or two. Do not under-rate them. You may find yourself sharing thoughts and ideas with someone even for an hour which you realise at the time, or later, are important for you. Some of these ideas which could have been at the back of your mind for a long time now begin to crystallise. Experiences too come up unexpectedly and can be significant, if you are open to them. These passing friends and experiences are all part of developing and changing into a more mature person. A brief sexual experience can be transforming. You could easily find that by meeting and relating to new people you recognise and learn about 'unused' parts of yourself. It is events like these that make people say: 'Talking to him struck a chord in me' or 'Being with her drew me out'.

This can be a remarkable period of consolidation at a personal level. It helps us to recognise that we are incomplete in many ways and yet life's experiences and the people we meet have much to teach us. The question is: are we prepared to learn? Life at times is like a jigsaw puzzle in which the pieces are mixed up and have to be rearranged into a new picture. It becomes a task and responsibility to do this for yourself and overcome the various emotional and practical difficulties you find yourself in.

A strange kind of freedom now appears no matter what your circumstances. Time takes on a different meaning. You are presented with choices of what to do with your time. Patterns change. At one extreme you may want to withdraw and stay at home night after night. At the other you may go out every night and fill all your spare time by socialising. Either way you may feel very much alone and even the freedom to do what you want may not dispel this state of mind. You have potentially the emotional freedom and perhaps the physical freedom to do as you please. We acknowledge the practical difficulties in finding a new life, particularly for a mother or father tied to the home and children. Remember that some kind of balance that keeps a thread of normal activities going will be a stabilising influence. Nevertheless, to turn some of your energy towards a new life will help create it.

A relationship break-up is one of life's crises in which an opportunity is given to build up increasing confidence in who you are and what you want to do. If you can work through the difficulties of this transition period and meet the challenge of the future you will experience an increasing sense of completeness. This embraces an awareness of what you need and want in life together with the development of those qualities which have not been fully expressed. This can bring a new kind of tolerance, sensitivity and caring, and equally a firmness in dealing with people, born of an increasing strength within. These are some of the other sides of ourselves we have to find. It is part of the process we have talked about throughout the book, a stage in the journey that is life itself.

Conclusions

'When we attended, we both listened to each other's comments and that was a first.' 'I was able to say what I felt and not be frightened.' These two comments, from people who were helped by mediation in Scotland, sum up a change that would have been hard to imagine not that many years ago. There is now skilled help on hand, widely available, when two people are in difficulties or divorce.

When we first wrote this book we complained that people were not being prepared for marriage. We quoted a counsellor, Betty Rubinstein, who said the lack of preparation for marriage was 'like launching a ship without lifeboats although it is known there are rocks ahead'. It is still true that very many couples who marry or live together make their commitment unaware of the skills they need to cope with the inevitable demands of maintaining their relationship.

Things have changed. More effort is being made to realise what marriage involves, and increase resources to help people rearrange their lives when their relationship is in trouble or has to end.

We are very heartened that, in many countries, creative arrangements are being encouraged for children's continuing involvement with both parents. Where parents themselves make the decisions instead of a court, a family's life can be transformed.

The thinking and expertise of professionals in the field – counsellors, mediators, lawyers and others – has become a driving force in helping this transformation. Some believe, for example, it is better for a divorcing couple to both move house when a relationship breaks up, rather than leave their children in the marital home with their mother. This 'traditional' solution, they argue, gives children a constant reminder of the family life they have lost and marginalises fathers. It can be made worse when the children visit him in his often dismal accommodation. At the same time, dependent mothers also are living with memories that hold them back. Working through such emotional obstacles, we believe, enables people to let go of past hurts, regain self-esteem and create a new life.

The problems of break-up and divorce reveal those inherent in many marriages; difficulties of communication and an imbalance of power leading to a lack of autonomy. This, says Christopher Clulow, director of the Tavistock Institute of Marital Studies, in London, has brought 'a burden of thwarted expectations which has led "intolerable disappointment" to replace "irretrievable breakdown" as the ground for divorce – especially for women'.

Today marriage is seen by marital therapists as a 'problematic relationship' which is not, as many people suppose, simply a place of comfort and security but a commitment that forces two people to resolve inevitable problems in order to grow. But there is more help available to manage these problems. For example, marriage preparation classes to improve communication skills, conflict-resolution teaching in schools, and the parenting plan developed in New Zealand.

So what can marriage be? We are sure that at its best – whether a couple is legally married or not – it is an intimate relationship that combines individuality with mutual growth and spiritual health. The spirit of exploration in relationships is creating a new climate in which the old rules are being re-examined. What the new pattern will be is not known yet.

We are, says Shere Hite (1994) in *The Hite Report on the Family*, 'on the threshold of eliminating emotional violence, redefining love and friendship, progressing in the area of children's rights and in men's questioning of their lives'. The two genders are beginning to understand each other better on a journey that will fascinate as it unfolds. The new pattern will be very different but one in which each person's potential has a greater chance of being realised.

Legal and mediation terms explained

These cover UK practice for England and Wales. Terms and definitions vary in Scotland, Northern Ireland and other parts of the world.

Legal terms

Acknowledgement of service   A form sent with the initial divorce papers (the petition) which asks whether the partner intends to oppose the divorce or not, and whether orders for children and costs are agreed or not.

Affidavit   A statement in writing on oath in support of a claim to the court; for example, for money orders. Ordinary statements, not sworn affidavits, are used in children's proceedings.

Affidavit in support of divorce petition   Statement which confirms statements in the petition and often includes the respondent's Acknowledgement of service.

Ancillary relief   The financial or property orders made by the court as part of the divorce arrangements. These can be settled in advance by two partners, or decided by the court after the decree nisi.

Answer   A defence in which a respondent denies allegations made in a divorce petition.

Application (or Summons)   A document from either partner asking for the court to make various orders relating to children or money, or an injunction to limit the other person's actions in some way.

Calderbank letter   Written offer of settlement which, if refused and the court does not make a better order, puts the person refusing at risk of paying some of the costs of the person making the offer.

Care/public law proceedings   When a local authority seeks orders concerning a child, including taking the child into care.

Chattels   Personal possessions, especially contents of a house; also a car.

Child of the family   Natural child of both spouses, or a child of one spouse but treated by the other as a natural child.

Child Support Agency   Government body that calculates amount of child maintenance by a strict formula. Also enforces unpaid court orders.

Clean break   A court order concerning finances where neither party has any further claims against the other, including continuing maintenance. A once-and-for-all settlement.

Cohabitation contract   Written agreement entered into by two people living together concerning their financial arrangements, interests in their home and (sometimes) living arrangements.

Community of property   System of law operated in many countries. Typically, assets acquired during marriage, sometimes excluding inheritances, are divided equally on divorce or death.

Conduct   Behaviour or action of one spouse which will be taken into account on financial issues. Rarely relevant now and considered by the court 'only where it is inequitable to disregard'.

Contact order   See *Court orders*.

Co-respondent   Person named in divorced proceedings as having committed adultery with the respondent. Co-respondent no longer need to be named in the UK.

Court orders   Orders made under the Children Act 1989 by the court when granting a divorce or at other times are:
    Contact order – Requires the person with whom a child lives to allow him/her to visit or stay with person named in the order. Includes letter or telephone contact, or supervised contact.
    Family assistance order – Short-term order (made with both parents' consent) enabling a court welfare officer or social services department to help and advise a family for six months.
    Prohibited steps order – States that no step, as specified, can be taken in relation to a child without the court's consent.
    Residence order – Names the person with whom a child, or children, is to live. (Both parents have responsibility for the child.)
    Specific issue order – Decides any dispute over a child's upbringing such as schooling, medical treatment or emigration.

Cross-petition   Statement in which the partner answering the divorce petition seeks a divorce for reasons of his or her own.

Decree nisi   Provisional granting by the court of a divorce which can be made final six weeks later provided the court is satisfied about arrangements for the children.

Decree absolute   The final granting of a divorce. This frees a person to remarry.

Directions for trial   Order made by the court to go ahead with the divorce hearing after receiving a request from the petitioner or his/her solicitor.

Disclosure   Each spouse has an obligation to give the court a full and frank disclosure of material and relevant matters.

Exhibit   Document such as a signed statement sent with the affidavit to give further information.

Filing   Process of lodging documents with the court for rubber-stamping and service on other parties.

Financial provision order   Court ruling allocating a family's finances as part of ancillary relief. May take the form of maintenance, a lump sum payment, transfer of property, settlements on children.

Green form   Government scheme to provide subsidised work by a solicitor for an uncomplicated divorce. Available to people on low incomes and limited capital.

In chambers   Private hearing by the court which only the couple and their lawyers can attend.

Injunction   Court order limiting the actions of a partner to protect the other partner. This can be quite specific: for example, preventing someone from molesting their partner or coming within a certain distance of the family home.

Judgement summons   An application to the court to reinforce an order, in extreme cases by imprisonment (called 'committal').

Judicial separation   Procedure enabling a couple to make their separation official but not divorcing them. The court has the same wide powers as in making divorce orders to grant settlements on children, money and property. Particularly used by people who do not agree with divorce.

Legal Aid   Scheme administered by the Legal Aid Board to provide the cost of legal work where there are matters in dispute which have to go to court. However, the costs may have to be paid by one or other of the partners; this can take the form of a charge over any property or other assets (called the statutory charge).

Maintenance order   The regular weekly or monthly payments a court orders one partner to pay the other for support of him/herself and children if there is no Child Support Agency assessment.

Marriage certificate   The original, or a certified copy or proper translation, which is filed at the court with the divorce petition.

Mediation   Family mediation is the process in which an impartial third person helps those involved in family breakdown (in particular separating and divorcing couples) to communicate better with one another and reach their own agreed and informed decisions about some or all of the issues arising over children, finance and property. Term now usually used instead of 'conciliation'.

Next friend   Adult who acts in court on behalf of a child. This may be a parent with whom the child lives, a legal guardian, or a social worker.

Non-molestation order Requires someone not to molest, interfere, assault or harrass another person.

Nullity   A decree granted by the court to end a marriage which is ruled invalid; for example, if one partner was already married to someone else (bigamy) or a marriage has not been consummated. The court has the same powers to make financial provision as in a valid marriage.

Ouster order   Requires someone to leave a property, usually after domestic violence, and not return. Also *Occupation order.*

Parental responsibility   All rights, duties, powers, responsibilities and authority that a parent has, in law, in relation to a child. Automatic for married parents and unmarried mothers. Unmarried fathers can acquire responsibility by court order or specific written agreement via the court. Does not end on divorce.

Party cited   Person named by the respondent to have committed adultery with the petitioner.

Penal notice   When attached to a court order, means the person named can be committed to prison if they break the order.

Periodical payments   A maintenance order.

Petition The papers which initiate divorce or judicial separation. They are lodged with the court by the person seeking the divorce (the petitioner) or by their solicitor. The court sends a copy to the partner (the respondent).

Petitioner The person who starts divorce proceedings by filing a petition with the court.

Prayer Claim in divorce petition for a divorce, or costs or other orders. A request.

Pre-marriage (or pre-nuptial) contract Written agreement made before marrying to deal with finances if there is a divorce. Not binding in English courts.

Prohibited steps order see *Court orders.*

Property adjustment order Ruling by the court to divide a family's capital assets such as a house. Part of ancillary relief.

Reconciliation Where a couple resolve their differences during or after divorce proceedings and are reunited.

Residence order see *Court orders.*

Respondent Person against whom the divorce or judicial separation action is brought.

Rule 2.63 questionnaire Written request for information and documents concerning the spouse's finances. From Family Proceedings Rules 1991.

Sealing Official stamping of documents filed at the court and of orders and decrees.

Section 8 orders Residence, contact, prohibited steps and specific issue orders. From Children Act 1989. See *Court orders.*

Section 41 certificate Shows court is satisfied with arrangements for children before decree absolute is granted. If not, it makes other orders.

Separation agreement Reached after separation to deal with finances and living arrangements. Probably binding if made with legal advice, disclosure and no duress.

Service Arrangement to give documents such as petitions and decrees to the parties for whom they are intended – by post or by handing them over personally.

Special procedure   The way a court decides if grounds for a divorce have been proven. No court hearing – the 'quickie' divorce.

Specific issue order   See *Court orders.*

Statement of arrangements   Form setting out arrangements proposed for the children, filed with the petition. Should be agreed in advance with the respondent if possible.

Undertaking   A personal commitment to the court and enforceable as if an order of the court.

Void/voidable marriage   Terms describing invalid marriages. A void marriage is one ruled to be non-existent, as in bigamy. A voidable marriage is one which has failed to be a legal union. Reasons can include that it is unconsummated, marriage under duress, or unfitness for marriage such as when a person is suffering from a statutory mental disorder when they marry.

Without prejudice   This is put on letters that make offers or compromises, so they cannot be shown to the court when deciding the case. Encourages settlement opportunities.

Mediation terms

All-issues (or comprehensive) mediation   Sessions which involve negotiations on property, finances as well as the future for children.

Budget sheet   Form on which a detailed statement of income and financial assets is given, or listing future financial needs. Used as a basis for discussion in mediation sessions.

Lawyer-mediator   A lawyer also trained in mediation skills.

Memorandum of understanding   Written 'agreement' arrived at when the issues have been talked through to a resolution. It is taken to a lawyer who, if satisfied it is reasonable for his or her client, turns it into a legal agreement for the divorce court to make into an order.

Parenting plan   A plan devised by parents for the future arrangements of their children, which is written down with details to fit a family's particular circumstances.

Organisations

Asian Family Counselling Service
Tel. 0181 997 5749

British Association of Counselling
Tel. 01788 550899

Child Poverty Action Group
Tel. 0171 253 3406; *fax* 0171 490 0561

Children Need Grandparents
2 Surrey Way, Laindon, Essex SS15 6PS
(enclose SAE)

Chinese Women's Refuge Group
Tel. 0171 837 7297

Citizens' Advice Bureau
See local phone book.

Council for Family Proceedings
(promoting interdisciplinary co-operation among professionals)
Tel. 0117 928 8136; *fax* 0117 974 1299

Families Need Fathers
Information line: *tel.* 0181 886 0970

Family Mediators Association (FMA)
Tel./fax 01225 465851

Gay and Lesbian Switchboard
Tel. 0171 837 7324; *fax*: 0171 837 7300

Get Advisory Service
(for Jewish religious divorce)
Tel. 0181 203 6314; *fax* 0181 203 8727

Gingerbread
(for lone parents)
Tel. 0171 240 0953; *fax* 0171 836 4500

Irchin
(forum for professionals on children's rights and welfare)
Tel./fax 0151 342 7852

Jewish Marriage Council
(offers counselling and mediation)
London: *tel.* 0181 203 6311; *fax* 0181 203 8727
Manchester: *tel.* 0161 795 1240

The Law Society
Tel. 0171 242 1222

Marriage Care
(former Catholic Marriage Advisory Council, offering counselling
and mediation)
Tel. 0171 371 1341; *fax* 0171 371 4921

National Council for One Parent Families
Tel. 0171 267 1361; 0171 482 4851

National Family Mediation
Tel. 0171 383 5993; *fax* 0171 383 5994

Network of Access & Child Contact Centres
Tel, 0115 9484557

Northern Ireland Women's Aid
Tel. 01232 249041; *fax* 01232 239296

Parentline
Tel. 01702 559900

Relate Marriage Guidance
See local phone book for counselling centres.
Relate's bookshop (*tel.* 01788 573241; *fax* 01788 535007) has a
mail-order booklist.

Relate Northern Ireland
Tel. 01232 323454

Solicitors Family Law Association
(members in England and Wales)
PO Box 302, Orpington, Kent BR6 8QX
Tel. 01689 850227

Southall Black Sisters
(counselling for black and Asian women)
Tel. 0181 571 9595

Stepfamily (National Stepfamily Association)
Tel. 0171 209 2460; *Counselling line* 0171 209 2464

UK College of Family Mediators
(sets standards under which FMA, NFM and FM Scotland operate.
Provides details of mediation services)
Tel. 0171 383 5993; *fax* 0171 383 5994

Welsh Women's Aid
Tel. 01222 390874

Women's Aid Federation
Tel. 0171 251 6537/8; *fax* 0171 608 0928; *Helpline* 0117 963 3542

THE UK – SCOTLAND

Citizens' Advice Bureau
Tel. 0131 557 1500

Family Mediation Scotland/Child Contact Centres
Tel. 0131 220 1610; *fax* 0131 220 6895

Marriage Counselling Scotland
Tel. 0131 225 5006; *fax* 0131 220 0639

One Plus
(for lone parents)
Tel. 0141 333 1450; *fax* 0141 333 1399

Scottish Women's Aid
Tel. 0131 229 1419; *fax* 0131 221 0402

REPUBLIC OF IRELAND

Accord (Catholic Marriage Counselling Service)
Tel. 01 837 5649/478 0866

Family Mediation Service
Tel. 01 872 8277/8708/8475; *fax* 01 878 7497

Irish Association of Counselling
Tel. 01 230 0061

Marriage Counselling Service
Tel. 01 872 0341

Women's Aid
Tel. 01 860 3033
Helpline: *Tel.* 800 341 900

AUSTRALIA

Relationships Australia
(counselling and mediation)
Adelaide, SA
Tel. 08 223 4566; *fax* 08 232 2898
Brisbane, Qld
Tel. 07 839 9144; *fax* 07 832 4864
Canberra, NSW
Tel. 06 281 3600; *fax* 06 281 3911
Darwin, NT
(counselling only)
Tel. 089 81 6676; *fax* 089 81 6190
Melbourne, Vic
Tel. 039 853 5354; *fax* 039 853 9158
Perth, WA
Tel. 09 470 5109; *fax* 09 470 5139
Sydney, NSW
Tel. 02 418 8800; *fax* 02 418 8725
Hobart, Tasmania
Tel. 002 313 141; *fax* 002 343 113

Family Court of Western Australia
(counselling and mediation; also mediation by telephone)
Tel. 09 224 8222/8366; *fax* 09 224 8360

Perth Child Contact Centres
Anglicare Perth. *Tel.* 09 321 7033

CANADA

Alberta Association for Marriage & Family Therapy
Tel. 403 448 9497

Family Mediation Canada/Mediation Familiale du Canada
Tel. 519 836 7750; *fax* 519 836 7204

Grandparents Requesting Access & Dignity Society
Tel. 613 837 8371

Kids First Parent Association of Canada
Tel. 403 289 1440

One Parent Families Association of Canada
Tel. 416 226 0062

Ontario Association for Marriage & Family Therapy
Tel. 800 267 2638

Parents Without Partners
Tel. 905 436 2255

NEW ZEALAND

Arbitrators and Mediators Institute of New Zealand
Tel. 9 630 6365

Department for Courts
(counselling and mediation conferences)
PO Box 2750, Wellington
Tel. 4 915 8300

Law Society of New Zealand
Tel. 4 372 7837

New Zealand Association of Counsellors
PO Box 165, Hamilton
Tel./fax 7 847 8974

New Zealand Family Court
(counselling, mediation conferences)
Tel. 4 915 8000

Relationship Services
(counselling, mediation)
Tel. 4 472 8798; *fax* 4 472 8507

SWEDEN

Familjerådgivningsbryån
(Family Counselling Bureau)
See local phone book.

Familjërattsbyrån
(Municipal Family Law Bureau – for mediation)
See local phone book.

Svenska Kyrkan Familjerådgivning
(Swedish Church Family Counselling)
Tel. 018 169500; *fax* 018 169703

Local authority (*kommun*) services provide information and advice.

UNITED STATES

Academy of Family Mediators
Massachusctts: *Tel.* 617 674 2663; *fax* 617 674 2690
(provides names of private mediators throughout the US and
internationally – 3,000 members worldwide). Mail-order booklist.

American Bar Association
(dispute resolution section)
Tel. 202 662 1680/1681

American Counselling Association
Tel. 703 823 9800

Association of Family and Conciliation Courts
Tel. 804 253 2000

Children's Rights Council
(information on parenting issues, finding counsellors, mediators and lawyers)
Tel. 202 547 6227; *fax* 202 546 4272

Divorce Care
Tel. 919 571 7735

Fresh Start
(divorce recovery workshops)
Tel. 800 882 2799

National Association of Social Workers
Tel. 800 638 8799

Parents Sharing Custody
(help and advice)
Tel. 310 286 9171; *fax* 310 551 1884

Step Family Association of America
Tel. 800 735 0329

Bibliography

Ahrons, Constance R. and Rodgers, Roy H. (1987) *Divorced Families – A Multidisciplinary Developmental View*, Norton.

Chandler, Joan (1991) *Women Without Husbands – An Exploration of the Margins of Marriage*, Macmillan.

Children Act 1989, HMSO, London.

Clulow, Christopher (ed.) (1993) *Rethinking Marriage – Public and Private Perspectives*, Karnac Books.

Clulow, Christopher (ed.) (1995) *Women, Men and Marriage – Talks from the Tavistock Marital Studies Institute*, Sheldon Press.

Costello, John (1985) *Love, Sex and War – Changing Values 1939–45*, Collins.

Davis, Gwynn (1982) Settlement-seeking in divorce, *New Law Journal*, 8 April.

Dyer, Wayne W. (1977) *Your Erroneous Zones*, Sphere.

Families Need Fathers (1995) *Divorce Law – Parliament, Practice and Pretence*.

Fensterheim, Herbert and Baer, Jean (1976) *Don't Say Yes When You Want to Say No*, Futura.

Friedan, Betty (1965) *The Feminine Mystique*, Penguin.

Friedan, Betty (1982) *The Second Stage*, Michael Joseph.

Fromm, Erich (1975) *The Art of Loving*, Unwin.

Furlong, Monica (1981) *Divorce – One Woman's View*, The Mothers' Union.

Garwood, Fiona (1989) *Children in Conciliation*, Family Mediation Scotland.

Gingerbread (1982) *Divided Children*.

Greene, Liz (1980) *Saturn – A New Look at an Old Devil*, Aquarian Press.

Greer, Germaine (1972) *The Female Eunuch*, Panther.

Guggenbühl-Craig, Adolf (1977) *Marriage Dead or Alive*, Spring Publications.

Hafner, Dr Julian (1993) *The End of Marriage – Why Monogamy Isn't Working*, Century.

Hannah, Barbara (1977) *Jung, His Life and Work*, Coventure.

Hite, Shere (1994) *The Hite Report on the Family*, Sceptre.

Hooper, Douglas and Dryden, Windy (eds) (1991) *Couple Therapy – A Handbook*, Open University Press.

Jacobi, Jolande (1981) *The Psychology of C.G. Jung*, Routledge.

Johnson, Robert A. (1977a) *He – Understanding Masculine Psychology*, Perennial Library, Harper & Row.

Johnson, Robert A. (1977b) *She – Understanding Feminine Psychology*, Perennial Library, Harper & Row.

Jones, Ernest (1964) *The Life and Work of Sigmund Freud*, Pelican.

Jong, Erica (1995) *Fear of Fifty*, Vintage.

Jung, C.G. (1972) *Four Archetypes*, Routledge & Kegan Paul.

Kassorla, Dr Irene (1973) *Putting It All Together*, Warner.

Kelly, Joan B. (1991) Parent interaction after divorce: comparison of mediated and adversarial divorce processes, *Behavioural Sciences and the Law* 9.

Kelly, Joan B. (1993) Current research on children's post-divorce adjustment – no simple answers, *Family and Conciliation Courts Review* 31(1), January.

Kelly, Joan B. (1994) The determination of child custody, *Children and Divorce* 4(1).

Kroll, Brynna (1994) *Chasing Rainbows – Divorce, Children and Loss*, Russell House.

Kupfermann, Jeannette (1981) *The MsTaken Body*, Paladin Granada.

Lawson, Annette (1995) in *Women, Men and Marriage – Talks from the Tavistock Marital Studies Institute*, ed. Christopher Clulow, Sheldon Press.

Looking to the Future – Mediation and the Ground for Divorce, HMSO, London, 1995.

Maslow, Abraham (1973) *The Farther Reaches of Human Nature*, Pelican.

McAllister, Fiona M., Mansfield, Penny and Dormor, Duncan J. (1991) Expectations and experience of marriage today, *Journal of Social Work Practice* 5(2).

McManus, Michael J. (1995) *Marriage Savers – Helping Your Friends and Family Avoid Divorce*, Zondervan.

Metzner, Ralph (1971) *Maps of Consciousness – Six Guides to Growth and Individuality*, Collier Books.

National Family Mediation (1995) *A Conciliator's Guide to the Children Act*.

Nicholson, Joyce (1977) *What Society Does to Girls*, Virago.

Oakley, Ann (1980) *Women Confined*, Martin Robertson.

O'Neill, George and Nena (1973) *Open Marriage*, Peter Owen.

Parkinson, Lisa (1994) in *Couple Therapy*, ed. Douglas Hooper and Windy Dryden, Open University Press.

Parkinson, Lisa (1995a) Divorce mediation – some issues of empowerment and control, *Family Law Journal*, November.

Parkinson, Lisa (1995b) The development of family mediation and regulation of practice, paper given at the International Bar Association Conference, Edinburgh.

Powell, John (1974) *The Secret of Staying in Love*, Argus Communications.

Powell, John (1975) *Why Am I Afraid to Tell You Who I Am?* Fontana.

Pryde, Duncan (1972) *Nunaga – Ten Years of Eskimo Life*, Corgi.

Quinn, Kaleghl (1983) *Stand Your Ground – A Woman's Guide to Self-preservation*, Orbis.

Roberts, Ceridwen (1995) in *Women, Men and Marriage – Talks from the Tavistock Marital Studies Institute*, ed. Christopher Clulow, Sheldon Press.

Scottish Law Commission (1991) *Confidentiality in Family Mediation* – Discussion paper no. 92.

Shirley, Steve (1995) Getting the Gender Issue on to the Agenda, *Professional Manager*, January.

Smedes, Lewis (1976) *Sex for Christians*, Triangle.

Solicitors Family Law Association (1995a) *Divorce Reform and Mediation – the Search for Fair Solutions*.

Solicitors Family Law Association (1995b) *Ways and Means – Legal Aid and Family Law*.

von Franz, Marie-Louise (1970) *Puer Aeternus*, Sigo Press.

Walker, Janet, McCarthy, Peter and Timms, Noel (1994) *Mediation: The Making and Remaking of Co-operative Relationships*, Relate Centre for Family Studies, University of Newcastle.

Welburn, Vivienne (1980) *Postnatal Depression*, Fontana.

West-Meads, Zelda (1995) *The Trouble With You – How Men and Women Can Learn to Understand Each Other*, Hodder & Stoughton.

Wickes, Frances G. (1977) *The Inner World of Childhood*, Coventure.